VOYAGES IN ENGLISH
WRITING AND GRAMMAR

Introduction

How This Practice Book and Assessment Book Answer Key Works

For your convenience, each Voyages in English Answer Key is a single but separate volume. This design allows you to grade papers without the need to carry and manage a complete Teacher Guide.

Inside each key you will find the annotated reduced pages from the Practice Book and the Assessment Book for an entire grade level. Two reduced pages appear on a single answer key page. The Practice Book pages, which are accessed more frequently, precede the Assessment Book pages. A description of the Practice Book and how it works follows on page 4. A similar introduction to the Assessment Book is provided on page 76.

Voyages in English and *Exercises in English* Grammar Correlation Charts

Included on pages 114–120 of this Answer Key are correlation charts for anyone who uses both *Voyages in English* and *Exercises in English*. These charts list each grammar section of *Voyages in English* and its corresponding lesson in *Exercises in English*. They provide users with a quick, easy reference to the content in Grades 3–8 for both programs.

VIE Section	EIE Lesson	VIE Section	EIE Lesson	VIE Section	EIE Lesson
Sentences		**Adjectives**		**Adverbs and Conjunctions**	
1.1	1	4.1	46–47		
1.2	2–3	4.2	48	6.1	84–85
1.3	4–5	4.3	49	6.2	86–87
1.4	6	4.4	50	6.3	88
1.5	7–8	4.5	51	6.4	89
1.6	9	4.6	52	6.5	90
1.7	10	4.7	53	6.6	91
1.8	11	4.8	54	Adverb and Conjunction Challenge	92
1.9	12	4.9	55		
1.10	13	4.10	56		
1.11	14	4.11	57	**Punctuation and Capitalization**	
Sentence Challenge	15	Adjective Challenge	58	7.1	93–94
Nouns		**Verbs**		7.2	95
2.1	16	5.1	59–60	7.3	96
2.2	17	5.2	61	7.4	97
2.3	18–19	5.3	62	7.5	98
2.4	20	5.4	63	7.6	99–102
2.5	21–22	5.5	64	7.7	103–104
2.6	23–24	5.6	65–66	7.8	105
2.7	25	5.7	67–68	7.9	106
2.8	26	5.8	69–71	Punctuation and Capitalization Challenge	107
2.9	27	5.9	72		
2.10	28	5.10	73		
2.11	29	5.11	74	**Diagramming**	
Noun Challenge	30	5.12	75–76	8.1	108
		5.13	77	8.2	109
Pronouns		5.14	78	8.3	110
3.1	31	5.15	79	8.4	111
3.2	32–34	5.16	80–81	8.5	112
3.3	35	5.17	82	8.6	113
3.4	36	Verb Challenge	83	8.7	114
3.5	37			8.8	115
3.6	38			8.9	116
3.7	39			8.10	117
3.8	40			Diagramming Challenge	118
3.9	41				
3.10	42–43				
3.11	44				
Pronoun Challenge	45				

Practice Book

Answer Key

4

VOYAGES

IN ENGLISH

Writing and Grammar

How the Practice Books Work

Fully integrated into the Voyages in English program, the Practice Book pages run parallel with the writing chapters and the grammar sections, providing additional work with the grammar and writing concepts covered in each chapter. Teachers use the Practice Book lessons as student homework and for reteaching and reinforcement, according to the needs of their students.

Every two-day lesson in each of the eight genre chapters of the Voyages Teacher Guide and Student Book is supported by three Practice Book pages—two that reinforce, reassess, or reteach the concepts assessed in the daily Focus on Grammar quiz and one that reinforces the characteristics of the genre or the skills taught in the lesson. These three Practice Book pages are clearly labeled to show how they correlate to the writing chapter or the parallel grammar section that is part of the integrated study. The Self-Assessment at the end of every chapter allows students to evaluate how well they mastered the writing and grammar content.

The Practice Book offers 17 pages of rigorous reinforcement per student book chapter: 2 genre lessons, 3 skills lessons, 11 grammar lessons, and a self-assessment writing and grammar rubric.

Practice Book Rubrics

Each Practice Book page offers reinforcement for students who had trouble mastering the lessons' writing and grammar skills.

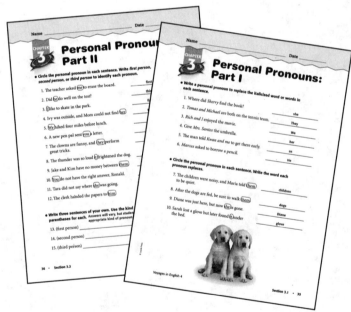

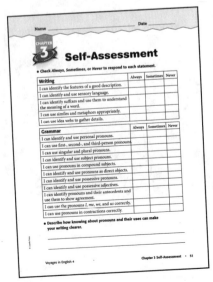

An additional student self-assessment tool, found in the Practice Book, allows young writers to see how well they have mastered the chapter content.

CHAPTER 1

Sentences: Part II

• **Add periods to the end of declarative sentences. Add question marks to the end of interrogative sentences.**

1. Where did your family go last weekend**?**
2. We hiked up the mountain**.**
3. How old will you be on your next birthday**?**
4. What is your favorite school subject**?**
5. Atlanta is the capital of Georgia**.**
6. Daniel wrote an excellent science report**.**
7. Do you like ice cream cake**?**
8. Randy believes the boots are in the closet**.**
9. The yo-yo appears to be broken**.**
10. Who is going to the store with me**?**

• **Write declarative sentences to answer the questions you identified above.**

11. ___ Answers will vary, but sentences should answer the questions from
12. ___ items 1, 3, 4, 7, and 10 and should end with a period.
13. _____
14. _____
15. _____

CHAPTER 1

Sentences: Part I

• **Write *sentence* or *not a sentence* to identify each group of words.**

1. An octopus has eight tentacles.   **sentence**
2. Spotted a bald eagle.   **not a sentence**
3. A rabbit hopped across the lawn.   **sentence**
4. My mother works at the museum.   **sentence**
5. Trails through forests and fields.   **not a sentence**
6. Flooded the valley.   **not a sentence**
7. The children ate hamburgers.   **sentence**
8. The forest ranger handed us a map.   **sentence**

• **Add words to the sentence fragments above to make each a complete sentence. Write your sentences on the lines below.**

9. Answers will vary, but students should rewrite items 2, 5, and 6 as complete sentences.
10. _____
11. _____

CHAPTER 1 — What Makes a Good Personal Narrative?

Name _____ Date _____

• Circle the letter of the phrase that best completes each sentence.

1. A personal narrative is a true story that tells
   (a.) about an event that really happened to the writer.
   b. about a person who lived over one hundred years ago.

2. Words like *I*, *me*, *we*, and *our* indicate that the writing is written in
   a. the third-person point of view.
   (b.) the first-person point of view.

3. The events in a personal narrative are
   a. made up so that they are more interesting.
   (b.) told in the order they happened using time words.

4. When you choose a topic for a personal narrative,
   (a.) write about an event that will be interesting to your audience.
   b. write about sports because everyone finds them interesting.

5. A good topic for a personal narrative is
   a. a list of facts and dates that tell everything that happened in your life.
   (b.) an event that really happened that was funny, exciting, or unusual.

Voyages in English 4   Lesson 1 • 3

© Loyola Press

CHAPTER 1 — Sentences: Part III

Name _____ Date _____

• Add periods to the end of imperative sentences. Add exclamation points to the end of exclamatory sentences.

1. How high the tower is!

2. Fasten your seatbelt.

3. I cannot believe you would say that!

4. Do not talk with your mouth full, please.

5. Please hand me that book.

6. Oh, the sunset is so beautiful!

7. Please turn off the water.

8. Take good care of my rabbit.

9. Oh no, the water level is rising!

10. Quiet the students in the library.

11. Check the doors before you leave.

12. Let's go dancing tonight!

• You are working with a partner on an art project in school. Write one imperative sentence and one exclamatory sentence you might say.

13. imperative

Answers will vary, but students should write the kind of sentence asked for.

14. exclamatory

4 • Section 1.3   Voyages in English 4

© Loyola Press

CHAPTER 1

Subjects and Predicates: Part I

- Draw one line under the complete subject in each sentence. Draw two lines under the complete predicate.

1. The wind howled.
2. Amy dropped the ball.
3. The hungry dog barked.
4. Elevators go up and down.
5. Carolina runs fast.
6. The old computer hummed.
7. Whales are mammals.
8. Jake found a dollar bill.
9. The small gray cat ran under the bed.
10. Coffee spilled on the table.
11. Thomas lost his wallet.
12. The teacher called my name.

- Write a complete subject or a complete predicate to complete each sentence.

13. _____ Answers will vary. _____ went to skateboard in the park.
14. _____ have green skin.
15. Two clowns _____.
16. A sandwich _____.

CHAPTER 1

Introduction, Body, and Conclusion

- For each set of sentences write *introduction, body,* or *conclusion* to tell the best place for each sentence in a personal narrative.

1. a. Little did I know what this day would hold. **introduction**
   b. This party was the best surprise of my life! **conclusion**
   c. I went to soccer practice as usual. **body**

2. a. In the end, I realized my dad had been right. **conclusion**
   b. By 11:00 all the numbers seemed to look the same. **body**
   c. My dad warned me not to put off studying to the last minute. **introduction**

3. a. I found the second clue a minute later. **body**
   b. This Saturday my family hosted their annual treasure hunt. **introduction**
   c. Perhaps my prize proves I am the best detective around! **conclusion**

4. a. As I splashed into the pool, I was relieved the ride was over. **conclusion**
   b. From the top of the waterslide, I was on top of the world. **introduction**
   c. My legs flew up as the first turn cast me sideways. **body**

CHAPTER 1

Compound Subjects

• Write *simple* or *compound* to identify the subject in each sentence.

1. Spring and fall are my favorite seasons. ___compound___

2. Santiago and Patrick are best friends. ___compound___

3. The library is closed on Wednesdays. ___simple___

4. A pencil and a pen are on the desk. ___compound___

5. The boys played tennis last night. ___simple___

6. Jennifer and Liz fed the chickens. ___compound___

7. My bat and ball are in this bag. ___compound___

8. People cheered for the winning team. ___simple___

• Add a compound subject to complete each sentence.

9. _____ and _____ make good pets.

10. The _____ and _____ are near my house.

11. _____ and _____ live in a desert.

12. _____ and _____ are the choices for lunch.

Answers will vary, but students should use subjects that fit in the context of the sentence.

CHAPTER 1

Subjects and Predicates: Part II

• Use a simple subject from the word box to complete each sentence. Then circle the simple predicate in each sentence.

puppies	artist	librarian	pencil	smoke
milk	pond	band	rug	tires

1. Our __librarian__ (showed) us the new book.

2. My __pencil__ (rolled) off my desk.

3. The __puppies__ (chase) the ball.

4. A new __rug__ (covered) the floor.

5. The __artist__ (painted) a picture.

6. The car __tires__ (screeched)

7. Black __smoke__ (rose) from the campfire.

8. This __pond__ (freezes) in the winter.

9. The __band__ (played) a marching song.

10. The __milk__ (costs) $1.50 a quart.

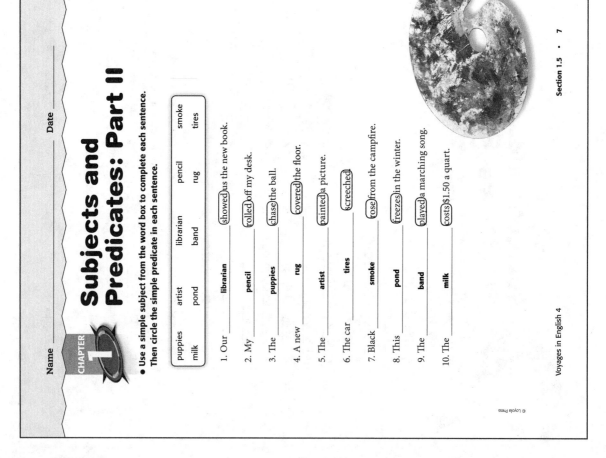

CHAPTER 1

Compound Predicates

• Underline the simple predicate or predicates in each sentence. Then write *simple* or *compound* to identify the predicate.

1. The wind <u>pounded</u> and <u>rattled</u> the windows. **compound**

2. Maria <u>ran</u> and <u>jumped</u> in the water. **compound**

3. We <u>picked</u> and <u>sorted</u> apples. **compound**

4. My little brother <u>colors</u> every afternoon. **simple**

5. Tom <u>broke</u> the table and later <u>fixed</u> it. **compound**

6. My cat <u>sniffed</u> its food and <u>walked</u> away. **compound**

7. Helen <u>smiled</u> and <u>laughed</u> at the clown. **compound**

8. The dog <u>growled</u> at the stranger. **simple**

• Add a compound predicate to complete each sentence.

9. The audience _____ and _____

10. The children _____ and _____ in the park.

11. We _____ our sandwich and _____ our fruit juice.

12. My aunt and uncle _____ and _____ in Denver.

Answers will vary, but students should use simple predicates that fit in the context of the sentence.

10 • Section 1.7

Voyages in English 4

CHAPTER 1

Time Lines

• Recall a day in your life when something interesting, funny, or scary happened. Use the time line to organize the events of that day.

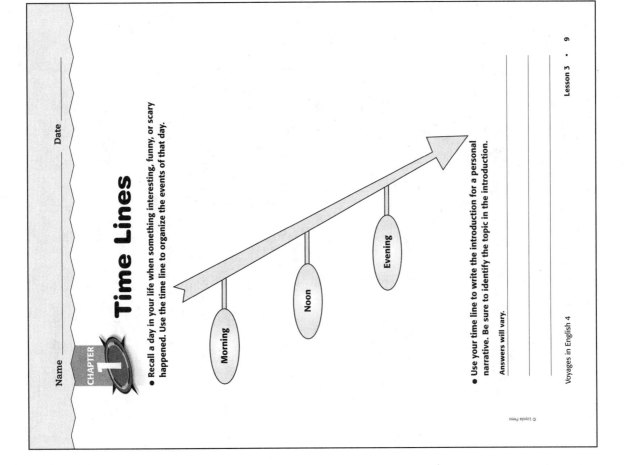

Morning

Noon

Evening

• Use your time line to write the introduction for a personal narrative. Be sure to identify the topic in the introduction.

Answers will vary.

_____

Voyages in English 4

Lesson 3 • 9

CHAPTER 1 — Direct Objects

Name _____ Date _____

Write the direct object of each sentence.

1. Cats love catnip. _____ catnip

2. Mrs. Lee grows flowers. _____ flowers

3. My brother watered the plants. _____ plants

4. Max sharpened his pencils. _____ pencils

5. Rosa painted a picture yesterday. _____ picture

6. Al rides his bicycle to school. _____ bicycle

7. Duncan and his brother raise pigeons. _____ pigeons

8. Our team easily won the game. _____ game

9. My father bought groceries for the week. _____ groceries

10. She found our route on a map. _____ route

11. The explorer discovered an island. _____ island

12. Ana and I each ate an apple. _____ apple

Write a direct object to complete each sentence. You can use other words with the direct object. Answers will vary.

13. My sister cooked _____.

14. Yesterday I saw _____.

15. We'll watch _____.

CHAPTER 1 — Exact Words

Name _____ Date _____

Use a word from the word box to replace each italicized word with a more exact word. Write the new word on the line.

fantastic	exclaimed	kindhearted
	darted	stroll

1. After dinner we decided to *walk* along the river. _____ stroll

2. My friend Teri is a very *nice* person. _____ kindhearted

3. "I think Dad found a nugget of gold!" I *said* excitedly. _____ exclaimed

4. When the deer saw us, it *went* into the forest. _____ darted

5. Our hike into the bat caves was a *good* trip. _____ fantastic

Complete the word web by writing more exact words for *big*. For an example of a word web see page 139. Answers will vary.

CHAPTER 1

Subject Complements

- Underline the simple subject in each sentence. Circle the subject complement.

1. I am the (baby sitter)
2. Those buildings are (tall)
3. A subway is an underground (train)
4. Paul has been (helpful)
5. The sun is (blinding)
6. Those pickles are very (sour)
7. Harry is my (cousin)

- Write a subject complement to complete each sentence.

8. Great white sharks are _____.
9. The concert this Saturday will be _____.
10. Yesterday's weather was _____.

Answers will vary, but complements should fit in the context of the sentence.

CHAPTER 1

Compound Sentences

- If the sentence is a compound sentence, circle the letter under *Yes*. If it is not, circle the letter under *No*.

	YES	NO
1. Jake painted the room, and Thomas cleaned the brushes.	(I)	T
2. Australia is a continent and a country.	O	(T)
3. The fireworks were loud and smelly.	P	(Q)
4. I ate a banana for lunch, and Ursula ate a sandwich.	(U)	E
5. The diver spotted the octopus, and the fisherman caught it.	(A)	O
6. The puppy was tired and hungry.	S	(C)
7. Bethany's room is green and yellow.	H	(K)
8. We found pennies under the bed, but Patrick spent them.	(S)	U
9. Dave eats spaghetti, and I eat ravioli.	(U)	M
10. Mom wants a new dress, but Dad bought a lawn mower.	(P)	E

- Now write the circled letters, in order, on the numbered lines below. If your answers are correct, you will reveal the answer to the riddle.

What happens to a duck when it flies upside down?

Answer:
I	T	Q	U	A	C	K	S	U	P
1	2	3	4	5	6	7	8	9	10

CHAPTER 1

Contractions with Pronouns

● Write the contraction for each pair of words.

1. I will	**I'll**	4. you have	**you've**
2. she is	**she's**	5. I would	**I'd**
3. they will	**they'll**	6. we are	**we're**

● These sentences are from a business letter. Circle the words or the contraction that correctly completes each sentence.

7. (I would) I'd) like to ask for the discount coupon.

8. I bought the toy in December and (it's (it is) already broken.

9. I hope you can attend our ceremony if (you are) you're) not busy.

● These sentences are from a letter to a friend. Circle the words or the contraction that correctly completes each sentence.

10. I thought (you'd) you would) like a photograph from the party.

11. My mom said (she will (she'll) drive us to the movie.

12. (It has (It's) been a long time since I last wrote.

Voyages in English 4

Lesson 5 • 15

CHAPTER 1

Run-On Sentences

● Write *correct* or *run-on* to identify each sentence.

1. Maria walks to school, her sister rides a bike.   **run-on**

2. Tonight is a new moon, and the stars will be very bright.   **correct**

3. The weather is cold today, the wind is icy.   **run-on**

4. I thought I was late, but the bus was early.   **correct**

5. Sherry wants a new book, she does not have enough money.   **run-on**

6. The children can play outside, they can watch a movie.   **run-on**

7. I can rake the leaves, or you can rake them for me.   **correct**

● Rewrite the run-on sentences from above as combined sentences. Students should rewrite items 1, 3, 5, and 6. Possible answers:

8. **Maria walks to school, but her sister rides a bike.**

9. **The weather is cold today, and the wind is icy.**

10. **Sherry wants a new book, but she does not have enough money.**

11. **The children can play outside, or they can watch a movie.**

16 •   Section 1.11

Voyages in English 4

Name _____ Date _____

- **Underline the nouns in each sentence. The number of nouns is in parentheses.**

1. <u>San Diego</u> is her favorite <u>city</u>. (2)

2. The <u>baby</u> cried and shook his <u>rattle</u>. (2)

3. My <u>grandfather</u> caught a <u>fish</u> in his <u>net</u>. (3)

4. <u>Rhode Island</u> is the smallest of the 50 <u>states</u>. (2)

5. <u>Lucy</u> found a shiny gold <u>coin</u>. (2)

6. <u>Abraham Lincoln</u> was our 16th <u>president</u>. (2)

7. Please buy some <u>carrots</u> at the <u>market</u>. (2)

8. My <u>family</u> rode a <u>raft</u> down the <u>American River</u>. (3)

- **Write each noun you underlined in the correct column of the chart.**

People	Places	Things
baby	**San Diego**	**rattle**
grandfather	**city**	**fish**
Lucy	**Rhode Island**	**net**
Abraham Lincoln	**states**	**coin**
president	**market**	**carrots**
family	**American River**	**raft**

Name _____ Date _____

- **Check *Always*, *Sometimes*, or *Never* to respond to each statement.**

Writing

	Always	Sometimes	Never
I can identify a personal narrative and its features.			
I can identify the introduction, body, and conclusion of a personal narrative.			
I can use a time line to organize information.			
I can identify and use exact words.			
I can identify and use contractions with pronouns.			

Grammar

	Always	Sometimes	Never
I can identify complete sentences.			
I can identify and punctuate the four types of sentences.			
I can identify and use complete subjects and predicates.			
I can identify and use simple subjects and predicates.			
I can identify and use compound subjects.			
I can identify and use compound predicates.			
I can identify and use direct objects in a sentence.			
I can identify and use subject complements.			
I can identify and use compound sentences.			
I can identify and avoid using run-on sentences.			

- **Describe how learning about sentences and their parts will help you be a better writer.**

_____

_____

CHAPTER 2

Common Nouns and Proper Nouns

● **Match each proper noun with a common noun. The first one is done for you.**

1. _f_ Memorial Day   a. country
2. _c_ March   b. mountain
3. _g_ Boston   c. month
4. _a_ France   d. river
5. _d_ Rio Grande   e. man
6. _b_ Mount Hood   f. holiday
7. _e_ William   g. city
8. _h_ Lake Erie   h. lake

● **Underline the nouns in each sentence. Then write _P_ for proper or _C_ for common above each noun to identify it.**

9. My <u>friend</u> moved from <u>Seattle</u> to <u>Memphis</u>.
     C   P   P

10. The <u>kangaroo</u> is a familiar <u>mammal</u> in <u>Australia</u>.
     C   C   P

11. <u>Lima</u> is the <u>capital</u> of <u>Peru</u> in <u>South America</u>.
   P   C   P   P

12. <u>Jones Beach</u> was crowded with <u>people</u>.
     P   C

CHAPTER 2

What Makes a Good Formal Letter?

● **Write _yes_ if the sentence is true or _no_ if it is false. Rewrite each false sentence so it is true.**

1. The heading of a letter is your own address with the date above it.   __no__

    Possible answer: The heading is your own address with the date below it.

2. The name and address of the person to receive the letter is called the inside address.   __yes__

3. The greeting of a letter should begin with _Dear_ and end with a period.   __no__

    Possible answer: The greeting should begin with _Dear_ and end with a colon.

4. The body is the part of the letter that explains why you are writing.   __yes__

5. A letter's closing should be short and polite.   __yes__

6. If you type your letter, you do not have to sign your name.   __no__

    Possible answer: If you type your letter, sign your name between the closing and your typed name.

7. It is correct to use contractions in a formal letter.   __no__

    Possible answer: Avoid using contractions in a formal letter.

8. You can close a letter with _Sincerely_ or _Respectfully_ followed by a comma.   __yes__

CHAPTER 2

Singular Nouns and Plural Nouns

● Write the plural form of each noun.

1. rock   **rocks**   6. key   **keys**

2. hose   **hoses**   7. baby   **babies**

3. dress   **dresses**   8. wish   **wishes**

4. peach   **peaches**   9. patch   **patches**

5. duty   **duties**   10. box   **boxes**

● Underline the nouns in each sentence. The number of nouns is in parentheses. Then write *S* for singular or *P* for plural above each noun to identify it.

11. <u>Saturn</u> is a <u>planet</u>. (2)
    S   S

12. The <u>students</u> sharpened their <u>pencils</u> before the <u>test</u>. (3)
        P   P   S

13. <u>Robert</u> washed the dirty <u>dishes</u>. (2)
   S   P

14. The <u>chest</u> was filled with <u>diamonds</u> and <u>rubies</u>. (3)
     S   P   P

15. This <u>store</u> also sells <u>watches</u>. (2)
     S   P

CHAPTER 2

Irregular Plural Nouns

● Write the correct plural form of the irregular noun in parentheses to complete each sentence.

1. Both **children** hit a home run. (child)

2. A gaggle of **geese** waddled across the road. (goose)

3. There were six **deer** grazing in the meadow. (deer)

4. How many **mice** do you have in the cage? (mouse)

5. A centipede has many **feet** . (foot)

6. A team of **oxen** pulled the wagon. (ox)

7. The child lost two **teeth** in December. (tooth)

8. It took four **men** to lift the heavy box. (man)

9. There were more **women** than men at the party. (woman)

10. How many **sheep** do you count before you sleep? (sheep)

● Use two of the irregular plural nouns you wrote in sentences of your own.

11. **Answers will vary.** _____

12. _____

Practice Book Answers • 15

Singular Possessive Nouns

Name _____ **Date** _____

CHAPTER 2

• Write the singular possessive form of the noun in parentheses to complete each sentence.

1. The ____coach's____ team has won seven games. (coach)

2. The ____boy's____ bicycle is in the garage. (boy)

3. ____Laura's____ money is in her piggy bank. (Laura)

4. Our ____dog's____ puppies are two weeks old. (dog)

5. My ____brother's____ room is never messy. (brother)

6. ____Mrs. Lincoln's____ classroom is down the hall. (Mrs. Lincoln)

• Circle the noun in each sentence that should be in singular possessive form. Then write the possessive form of the noun.

7. (Sharon) room is a mess! ____Sharon's____

8. A (turtle) shell protects it from enemies. ____turtle's____

9. (Mr. Jackson) house has a big porch. ____Mr. Jackson's____

10. I was invited to my (cousin) birthday party. ____cousin's____

11. The (baby) birthday is in December. ____baby's____

12. Brad put the paper on the (teacher) desk. ____teacher's____

© Loyola Press

24 • Section 2.5

Voyages in English 4

Types of Formal Letters

Name _____ **Date** _____

CHAPTER 2

• Read each sentence from a formal letter. Make a check mark under the correct heading to tell if the sentence would appear in a letter of complaint or in a letter of request.

	Complaint	Request
1. I am disappointed in the quality of the CD player.	✓	
2. Could you please send me a map of your city?		✓
3. I would like some brochures about tours.		✓
4. Can you provide some information about your factory?		✓
5. Please refund my money.	✓	
6. You will find five proof-of-purchase seals enclosed.		✓
7. After several tries, I still could not get the pen to write.	✓	
8. I have included a self-addressed, stamped envelope.		✓

• Rewrite each sentence using formal and polite language.

9. This is the stupidest tool I've ever had, and I'm telling everyone it stinks.

Answers will vary, but students should use a polite tone and avoid slang.

10. Your city is so awesome, and it would be cool if you could send me some stuff about it.

Answers will vary, but students should use more formal language.

© Loyola Press

Voyages in English 4

Lesson 2 • 23

16 • Voyages in English

CHAPTER 2

Compound Sentences

● Match each sentence in the first column with a related sentence in the second column. Write the matching letter on the line. The first one is done for you.

1. __c__ Butterflies have straight antennae with knobs at the ends.

2. __a__ We wanted to walk to the park.

3. __e__ Today Omar can ride his skateboard.

4. __b__ Stacy loves almonds.

5. __d__ Lightning flashed.

a. It was too cold.

b. She puts them on everything.

c. Moths have feathery ones.

d. Thunder shook the house.

e. He can go to the baseball game.

● Now rewrite each pair of sentences from above as a compound sentence on the lines below. Remember to use the correct conjunction.
Possible answers:

6. Butterflies have straight antennae with knobs at the ends, but moths have feathery ones.

7. We wanted to walk to the park, but it was too cold.

8. Today Omar can ride his skateboard, or he can go to the baseball game.

9. Stacy loves almonds, and she puts them on everything.

10. Lightning flashed, and thunder shook the house.

CHAPTER 2

Plural Possessive Nouns

● Circle the letter of the answer that shows the correct plural possessive form to complete each sentence.

1. The _____ sailing team won the race.
   a. womans'
   b. womens'
   (c) women's

2. The _____ clothes are in the closet.
   a. babys'
   (b) babies'
   c. babie's

3. We visited the _____ habitat at the zoo.
   (a) lions'
   b. lion's
   c. liones'

4. Do you see my _____ car?
   a. parent's
   (b) parents'
   c. parentes'

5. The _____ workshop meets today.
   (a) writers'
   b. writer's
   c. writers's

6. The _____ playground was just built.
   a. childs'
   b. childrens'
   (c) children's

7. The _____ brushes are in the sink.
   a. painter'
   b. painter'es
   (c) painters'

8. They studied many _____ paintings.
   a. artist's
   b. artistes'
   (c) artists'

9. _____ down feathers fill these pillows.
   a. Gooses'
   b. Geese'
   (c) Geese's

10. She cleaned the _____ cage today.
    (a) mice's
    b. mouses'
    c. mices'

CHAPTER 2

Count Nouns and Noncount Nouns

• Circle the letter under the heading that correctly identifies the italicized word as a count noun or a noncount noun.

	Count Noun	Noncount Noun
1. This jewelry *store* also sells watches.	(W)	M
2. The *weather* will be rainy on Monday.	U	(A)
3. The sound of *laughter* filled the room.	D	(T)
4. We planted new *grass* in our front yard.	D	(C)
5. The *sisters* stepped quickly over the hot sand.	(H)	Y
6. Michigan has many *lakes*.	(D)	P
7. *Sunshine* filled the empty rooms.	A	(O)
8. May I borrow a cup of *sugar*?	T	(G)

• Now write the circled letters, in order, on the numbered lines below. If your answers are correct, you will reveal the answer to the riddle.

What animal keeps the best time?

Answer: a W A T C H D O G
           1 2 3 4 5 6 7 8

CHAPTER 2

Collective Nouns

• Circle the collective noun in each sentence.

1. My family takes a trip to the Grand Canyon each year.
2. The audience watched the performance.
3. Our class wants to invite the mayor to our science fair.
4. His uncle showed us the litter of puppies.
5. A flock of swallows makes their nests here every season.
6. The herd of zebra drank at the watering hole.

• Now use the collective nouns you circled to complete the sentences below.

7. A __herd__ of cattle grazed on the green grass.
8. The __family__ had a picnic by the river.
9. My cat had a __litter__ of kittens last week.
10. At the end of the play, the __audience__ clapped loudly.
11. A __flock__ of seagulls landed near the water.
12. Does your __class__ have music after recess?

CHAPTER 2

Nouns as Subjects

● Circle the noun used as the subject in each sentence.

1. The (man) parked his car.

2. My (mom) fixed the broken light.

3. The (snow) fell silently.

4. (Luis) read a magazine.

5. My old (cat) sleeps most of the day.

6. (Mrs. Peters) teaches karate.

● Complete each sentence with a noun as the subject.

7. The _____ will end soon.

8. _____ walked home alone.

9. Our _____ rolled under the fence.

10. The _____ howled through the trees.

11. Many _____ watched the baseball game.

12. Her new _____ cost a lot of money.

Answers will vary, but students should use subject nouns that make sense within the context of the sentence.

© Loyola Press

CHAPTER 2

Mailing a Formal Letter

● Use the information below to address the envelope. Draw a stamp in the correct place.

Return address: James R. Thomas, 7670 Oak Avenue, Duluth, WA 98678
Mailing address: Ms. Terry Handry, President, Hoot Owl Books, 10 Emerald Road, Hollywood, CA 90023

James R. Thomas
7670 Oak Avenue
Duluth, WA 98678

| draw stamp here |

Ms. Terry Handry
President
Hoot Owl Books
10 Emerald Road
Hollywood, CA 90023

● Circle the correct abbreviation for the name of each state.

1. Pennsylvania (PA) PN   PV   PE
2. Missouri   MI   MS   MR (MO)
3. Nevada   NE (NV) NA   ND
4. Kentucky   KT   KE (KY) KK
5. Vermont   (VT) VR   VM   VE

© Loyola Press

CHAPTER 2 — Antonyms

- **Circle the word in each row that is an antonym for the italicized word.**

1. *old*	awful	ancient	funny	(young)
2. *difficult*	fast	hard	(easy)	rough
3. *narrow*	skinny	(wide)	high	weak
4. *neat*	(sloppy)	tidy	rocky	smooth
5. *slow*	(quick)	warm	right	awake
6. *first*	second	one	begin	(last)
7. *tired*	hungry	long	(energetic)	rich
8. *poor*	thin	(wealthy)	fast	thick

- **Choose two antonyms from above and use them to write a compound sentence.**

Example: The river is *wide*, but the stream is *narrow*.

Answers will vary.

_____

_____

- **Copy a word-analysis chart onto a separate piece of paper. Complete the chart for one of the antonyms from above. For an example of a word-analysis chart, see page 140.**

CHAPTER 2 — Nouns as Direct Objects

- **Circle the noun used as the direct object in each sentence.**

1. Will and Maria sang a (song).
2. The baby misses her (mother).
3. The audience applauded the (actor).
4. The two birds built a new (nest).
5. Linda wrote a (letter) to her grandmother.
6. On windy days I fly my (kite).
7. Shana introduced (Jill) to her friends.
8. I helped my best (friend) after school.
9. The children played a (game).
10. Devon read a (story) to his brother.

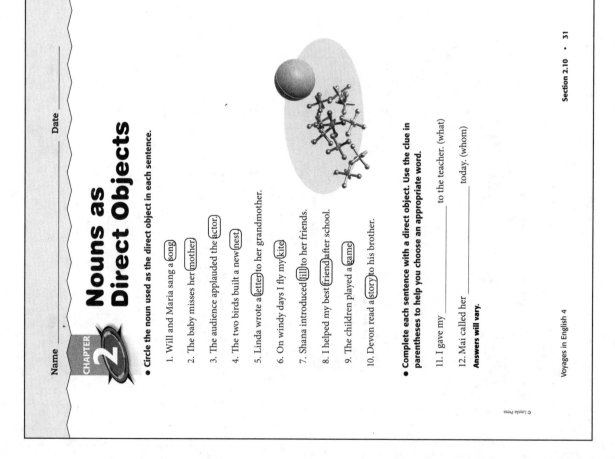

- **Complete each sentence with a direct object. Use the clue in parentheses to help you choose an appropriate word.**

11. I gave my _____ to the teacher. (what)

12. Mai called her _____ today. (whom)

Answers will vary.

CHAPTER 2 — Nouns as Subject Complements

• Circle the subject complement in each sentence. Underline the subject it tells more about.

1. The lifeguard is a good swimmer.

2. My cousins are soccer players.

3. The yellow marigolds are cheery flowers.

4. "The Grasshopper and the Ant" is a well-known fable.

5. Carlita is a girl in my class.

6. The principal is a big sports fan.

7. This tree is a maple.

8. The children are fourth graders.

9. This book was my favorite story.

10. China is a very large country.

11. Portland is a city in Oregon and Maine.

12. A cricket is an insect.

• Write a noun used as a subject complement to complete each sentence. You can use other words with the noun.

13. Poland is _____.

14. Dolphins are _____.

15. My favorite sport is _____.

Answers will vary.

CHAPTER 2 — Self-Assessment

• Check *Always, Sometimes,* or *Never* to respond to each statement.

Writing	Always	Sometimes	Never
I can identify a formal letter and its features.			
I can identify the types of formal letters.			
I can combine short sentences and use the correct conjunction to make compound sentences.			
I can mail a formal letter.			
I can identify and use antonyms.			

Grammar	Always	Sometimes	Never
I can identify and use nouns.			
I can identify and use common and proper nouns.			
I can correctly form and use singular and plural nouns.			
I can correctly form and use irregular plural nouns.			
I can correctly form and use singular possessive nouns.			
I can correctly form and use plural possessive nouns.			
I can identify and use collective nouns.			
I can identify and use count and noncount nouns.			
I can identify and use nouns as subjects.			
I can identify and use nouns as direct objects.			
I can identify and use nouns as subject complements.			

• **Explain how learning about nouns will help you be a better writer.**

_____

CHAPTER 3 · Personal Pronouns: Part I

Name _____ Date _____

- **Write a personal pronoun to replace the italicized word or words in each sentence.**

1. Where did *Sherry* find the book? — she
2. *Tomas and Michael* are both on the tennis team. — They
3. *Rich and I* enjoyed the movie. — We
4. Give *Mrs. Santos* the umbrella. — her
5. The man told *Kwan and me* to get there early. — us
6. *Marcus* asked to borrow a pencil. — He

- **Circle the personal pronoun in each sentence. Write the word each pronoun replaces.**

7. The children were noisy, and Maria told (them) to be quiet. — children
8. After the dogs are fed, be sure to walk (them). — dogs
9. Diane was just here, but now (she) is gone. — Diane
10. Sarah lost a glove but later found (it) under the bed. — glove

© Loyola Press

Section 3.1 • 35

Voyages in English 4

CHAPTER 3 · Personal Pronouns: Part II

Name _____ Date _____

- **Circle the personal pronoun in each sentence. Write *first person*, *second person*, or *third person* to identify each pronoun.**

1. The teacher asked (me) to erase the board. — first person
2. Did (he) do well on the test? — third person
3. (I) like to skate in the park. — first person
4. Ivy was outside, and Mom could not find (her). — third person
5. (We) hiked four miles before lunch. — first person
6. A new pen pal sent (you) a letter. — second person
7. The clowns are funny, and (they) perform great tricks. — third person
8. The thunder was so loud (it) frightened the dog. — third person
9. Jake and Kim have no money between (them). — third person
10. (You) do not have the right answer, Ronald. — second person
11. Tara did not say where (she) was going. — third person
12. The clerk handed the papers to (him). — third person

- **Write three sentences of your own. Use the kind of pronoun in parentheses for each. Answers will vary, but students should use the appropriate kind of pronoun in each sentence.**

13. (first person) _____
14. (second person) _____
15. (third person) _____

© Loyola Press

36 • Section 3.2

Voyages in English 4

CHAPTER 3

What Makes a Good Description?

● Use the words in the word box to complete the sentences. Use each word only once.

| organized | picture | senses | time |
| descriptive | audience | topic | describe |

1. Choose a __**topic**__ that is broad enough to describe but limited enough to write about in a given amount of __**time**__ .

2. __**Descriptive**__ writing helps readers clearly __**picture**__ people, places, things, and events.

3. Think about how much your __**audience**__ will know about the subject before you write.

4. Readers can more clearly picture a description if it is written in an __**organized**__ way.

5. You should only __**describe**__ things that you know well.

6. Use your five __**senses**__ to describe the subject in detail.

● Write *space order* or *time order* to identify the best way to organize each topic. Then circle one topic, and free write descriptive words and phrases about it on a separate sheet of paper.

7. a trip to the grocery store __**time order**__

8. a vase of flowers __**space order**__

9. your state flag __**space order**__

10. a walk through the park __**time order**__

Descriptive word lists will vary, but students should focus on one of the listed topics and use the correct order.

CHAPTER 3

Singular Pronouns and Plural Pronouns

● Rewrite each sentence, replacing the italicized word or words with a pronoun. Then write *singular* or *plural* to identify the pronoun.

1. *Domingo and I* cleared a path. __**plural**__

   We cleared a path.

2. *That cookie* was the last one in the jar! __**singular**__

   It was the last one in the jar!

3. The older children walked *the younger children* home. __**plural**__

   The older children walked them home.

4. Why is Jamie looking at *Jane and me?* __**plural**__

   Why is Jamie looking at us?

5. *Jim and Mickey* take the bus to school. __**plural**__

   They take the bus to school.

6. *Mei* showed the class a short film. __**singular**__

   She showed the class a short film.

7. *Rick* taught his brother how to tie knots. __**singular**__

   He taught his brother how to tie knots.

8. *The hamsters* are in a cage in Roberta's room. __**plural**__

   They are in a cage in Roberta's room.

CHAPTER 3 — Subject Pronouns

- **Circle the pronoun used as a subject in each sentence.**

1. (He) planted sunflowers in the garden.

2. What can (we) do with this garbage?

3. (You) should read more books.

4. (It) has spines for defense.

5. Do (they) like green vegetables?

- **Rewrite each sentence, replacing the subject noun with a pronoun.**

6. Early in the morning Kristen went swimming.

   Early in the morning she went swimming.

7. Ben and I always go to the beach in July.

   We always go to the beach in July.

8. Grandma saw a bear at the edge of the woods.

   She saw a bear at the edge of the woods.

9. The rain began in the early evening.

   It began in the early evening.

CHAPTER 3 — Sensory Language

- **Circle the letter of the sentence in each pair that uses sensory language.**

1. A. The kitten slept on the chair.
   (B.) Curled in a fuzzy ball, the kitten slept peacefully.

2. A. The raindrops fell and made the sidewalk wet.
   (B.) Circular splatters of rain dotted the gray concrete.

3. (A.) The black shadow of the big cat glided briefly into sight and then vanished.
   B. The jaguar moved swiftly and disappeared into the jungle.

4. A. The orange was juicy and sweet.
   (B.) The fruit's orange sweetness danced across my taste buds.

- **Rewrite each sentence using sensory details. Answers will vary.**

5. A truck shifted gears and drove down the street.

   _____

6. I will wrap the quilt around my shoulders.

   _____

7. The bacon and toast smelled good.

   _____

8. The heat from the sun makes her skin warm.

   _____

CHAPTER 3

Object Pronouns

- If the underlined pronoun is used as a direct object, circle the number under *Yes*. If the pronoun is not used as a direct object, circle the number under *No*.

	Yes	No
1. She carried <u>it</u> into the classroom.	(159)	154
2. <u>He</u> rang the bell each morning.	325	(300)
3. Jack embarrassed <u>her</u> with his bad behavior.	(505)	509
4. My mother cooked <u>them</u> for breakfast.	(298)	279
5. <u>We</u> painted pictures in the art class.	661	(616)
6. They helped <u>her</u> with the project.	(400)	500
7. Will <u>you</u> walk the dogs after school?	181	(118)
8. Thomas stopped <u>me</u> for a reason.	(64)	46

- Add together all the numbers you circled above. If your answers are correct, you will find the answer to the question below.

If you traveled on Interstate 10 from Santa Monica, California, to Jacksonville, Florida, approximately how many miles would you go?

2,460 miles

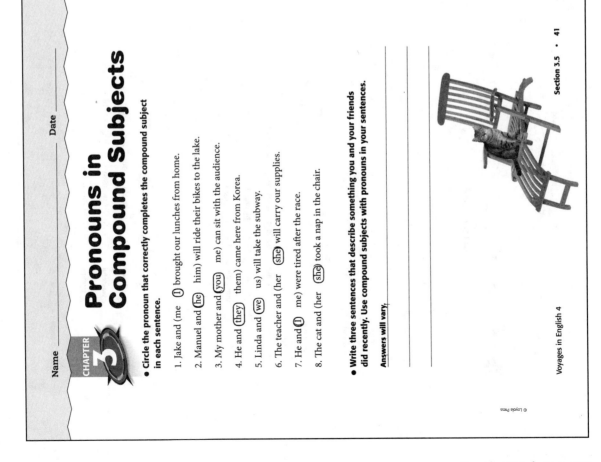

Santa Monica, CA

Jacksonville, FL

Voyages in English 4

© Loyola Press

CHAPTER 3

Pronouns in Compound Subjects

- Circle the pronoun that correctly completes the compound subject in each sentence.

1. Jake and (me   (I)) brought our lunches from home.
2. Manuel and ((he)   him) will ride their bikes to the lake.
3. My mother and ((you)   me) can sit with the audience.
4. He and ((they)   them) came here from Korea.
5. Linda and ((we)   us) will take the subway.
6. The teacher and (her   (she)) will carry our supplies.
7. He and ((I)   me) were tired after the race.
8. The cat and (her   (she)) took a nap in the chair.

- Write three sentences that describe something you and your friends did recently. Use compound subjects with pronouns in your sentences.

Answers will vary.

_____

_____

_____

Voyages in English 4

© Loyola Press

Panel 1: Possessive Pronouns

CHAPTER 3

Possessive Pronouns

- Underline the possessive noun phrase in each sentence. Rewrite the sentence, replacing the possessive noun with a possessive pronoun. The first one is done for you.

1. Did you find my baseball glove?

   Did you find mine?

2. Their school colors are blue and yellow.

   Theirs are blue and yellow.

3. The white rabbit is Sandra's.

   The white rabbit is hers.

4. We thought our show was on TV.

   We thought ours was on TV.

5. Who developed your pictures?

   Who developed yours?

6. The Jones's pool is built in the ground.

   Theirs is built in the ground.

7. Pedro keeps his music tapes in a box.

   Pedro keeps his in a box.

8. My family came here from Mexico.

   Mine came here from Mexico.

Panel 2: Suffixes

CHAPTER 3

Suffixes

- Write a word with a suffix that fits each meaning.

1. without thought   **thoughtless**
2. a person who paints   **painter**
3. a person who skis   **skier**
4. full of rocks   **rocky**
5. full of waste   **wasteful**
6. without care   **careless**
7. full of beauty   **beautiful**
8. like a grump   **grumpy**

- Use the words you wrote above to complete these sentences.

9. We gazed in awe at the **beautiful** sunset.
10. The **thoughtless** girl forgot to write a thank-you note for her gift.
11. I got the problem wrong because of a **careless** mistake.
12. The **skier** adjusted her goggles and took off down the white slope.
13. This soil is so **rocky** we keep digging up stones.
14. The **painter** covered the canvas with bright colors.
15. It is **wasteful** to throw away paper that can be used again.
16. I was **grumpy** this morning since I didn't get enough sleep.

CHAPTER 3

Possessive Adjectives

● Rewrite each group of words using a possessive adjective. The first one is done for you.

1. Thomas's map — his map

2. the gift that belongs to Enrique — **his gift**

3. bicycle that belongs to me — **my bicycle**

4. Michelle's report — **her report**

5. the children's toys — **their toys**

6. a pelican's nest — **its nest**

7. the car's tires — **its tires**

8. books that belong to my brothers and me — **our books**

9. a pencil that belongs to you — **your pencil**

10. rooms that belong to the guests and you — **your rooms**

11. the helmet that is mine — **my helmet**

12. the horse that is hers — **her horse**

● Choose two of the possessive adjective phrases you wrote. Write a sentence using each phrase. Answers will vary.

13. _____

14. _____

CHAPTER 3

Similes and Metaphors

● Write *simile* or *metaphor* to identify each description.

1. The peanut butter stuck to the roof of my mouth like wet cement. — **simile**

2. The moon is a silver ember that lights up the sky. — **metaphor**

3. The sound of the rain was a drumbeat on the window. — **metaphor**

4. The runner was as fast as a jackrabbit. — **simile**

5. The fireflies were like tiny flashlights in the dark garden. — **simile**

6. Our dreams are newborn birds waiting to fly. — **metaphor**

● Write a simile or metaphor to describe each subject.

7. an old shoe
   Answers will vary.

8. a field of blue flowers

9. seagulls waiting to be fed in a park

10. a child eating a hamburger quickly

Page 1 (right side):

Name _____ Date _____

CHAPTER 3

I, Me, We, and Us

• Circle the pronoun that correctly completes each sentence.

1. Mom took (I **me**) to the circus.
2. Bert and (**I** me) swam the length of the pool.
3. Our dad took (we **us**) out for breakfast.
4. On Saturday (**we** us) went ice skating.
5. Next September (**I** me) will enter fifth grade.
6. Mr. Swanson gave the award to Ines and (we **us**).
7. Melissa sent flowers to Aunt Lila and (I **me**).
8. (**We** Us) cheered for our team to win.
9. This music pleases (I **me**).
10. Mr. McGuire coaches (we **us**).
11. The movie surprised (we **us**).
12. The Hamaguchis and (**I** me) went to the city.

• Write three sentences that describe something you and your classmates did recently. Use these pronouns: *I, me, we, us.*

Answers will vary.

_____
_____
_____

48 • Section 3.10

Voyages in English 4

© Loyola Press

Page 2 (left side):

Name _____ Date _____

CHAPTER 3

Pronouns and Antecedents

• Circle the pronoun in each sentence. Draw an arrow to its antecedent.

1. Has Kiyoshi found the keys **he** lost?
2. My sister says **she** likes to study the stars.
3. The man said **he** enjoyed the trip to Egypt.
4. Mr. and Mrs. Williams invited guests and welcomed **them** at the door.
5. The seashore was beautiful, and my family enjoyed seeing **it**.
6. The beavers made a dam so **they** would be warm for the winter.
7. My brothers have the day off, and **they** want to play tennis.
8. My father suggested a game, and **he** wants to play too.
9. Take this star cutout and trace **it** on the paper.
10. The buildings are old and look as if **they** are falling down.

• Write a pronoun for the italicized antecedent to complete each sentence.

11. *The plane* is going to Seattle, and ____ **it** ____ will take off soon.
12. *Winston and Clyde* won the race, and ____ **they** ____ received a bronze trophy.

Voyages in English 4

Section 3.9 • 47

© Loyola Press

---

28 • Voyages in English

Name _____ Date _____

CHAPTER 3

Pronouns and Contractions

• Underline the words that can be replaced by a contraction with a pronoun in each sentence. Then write the contraction.

1. I am a good writer.   **I'm**

2. Mr. Wilson asked if you are ready.   **you're**

3. It is a beautiful day.   **It's**

4. We are walking to the lake today.   **We're**

5. They have finished the race in record time.   **They've**

6. I wonder if he is tired.   **he's**

7. Please let me know when you have finished your homework.   **you've**

8. We have read about the California missions.   **We've**

• Write at least three sentences that describe what you would like to do with your family on your next vacation. Include contractions with pronouns in your sentences.

Answers will vary.

_____

_____

_____

_____

_____

50 • Section 3.11   Voyages in English 4

Name _____ Date _____

CHAPTER 3

Idea Webs

• Think about a favorite place. Complete the idea web by listing details about that place. For an example of an idea web see page 139.

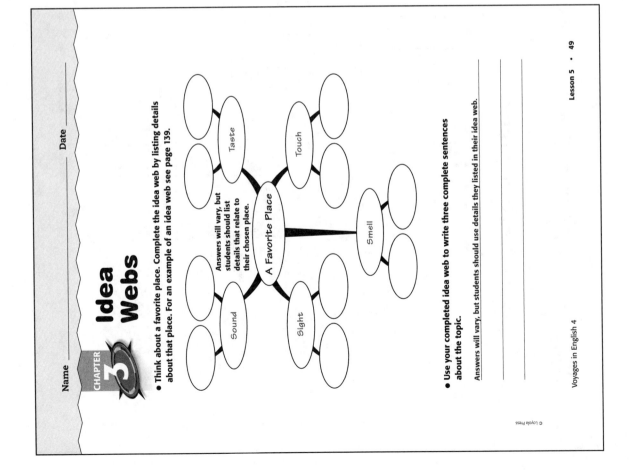

Answers will vary, but students should list details that relate to their chosen place.

(A Favorite Place — Taste, Touch, Smell, Sight, Sound)

• Use your completed idea web to write three complete sentences about the topic.

Answers will vary, but students should use details they listed in their idea web.

_____

_____

Voyages in English 4   Lesson 5 • 49

Practice Book Answers • **29**

Chapter 4 — Descriptive Adjectives

Name _____ Date _____

CHAPTER 4

Descriptive Adjectives

• Circle the descriptive adjectives in each sentence. Draw an arrow from each adjective to the noun it describes.

1. I wrote a (long) letter to Grandmother.

2. We saw the (talented) actor in a play.

3. The (clever) fox did not go out onto the (thin) ice.

4. The (upset) woman had lost a (valuable) bracelet.

5. The (striped) snake crawled through the (green) grass.

• Write a descriptive adjective before each noun to complete each sentence.

6. A _____ camper climbed up the _____ cliff.

7. We saw a _____ raccoon in a _____ tree.

8. The _____ door opened slowly to reveal a _____ figure.

9. The _____ thunder scared the _____ child.

10. _____ flames leapt from the _____ campfire.

Answers will vary.

52 • Section 4.1   Voyages in English 4

© Loyola Press

Chapter 3 — Self-Assessment

Name _____ Date _____

CHAPTER 3

Self-Assessment

• Check *Always*, *Sometimes*, or *Never* to respond to each statement.

Writing	Always	Sometimes	Never
I can identify the features of a good description.			
I can identify and use sensory language.			
I can identify suffixes and use them to understand the meaning of a word.			
I can use similes and metaphors appropriately.			
I can use idea webs to gather details.			

Grammar	Always	Sometimes	Never
I can identify and use personal pronouns.			
I can use first-, second-, and third-person pronouns.			
I can use singular and plural pronouns.			
I can identify and use subject pronouns.			
I can use pronouns in compound subjects.			
I can identify and use pronouns as direct objects.			
I can identify and use possessive pronouns.			
I can identify and use possessive adjectives.			
I can identify pronouns and their antecedents and use them to show agreement.			
I can use the pronouns *I, me, we,* and *us* correctly.			
I can use pronouns in contractions correctly.			

• Describe how knowing about pronouns and their uses can make your writing clearer.

_____

_____

Voyages in English 4   Chapter 3 Self-Assessment • 51

---

30 • Voyages in English

CHAPTER 4

Proper Adjectives

• Write the proper adjective formed from the proper noun in parentheses to complete each sentence. Check a dictionary for the correct spellings.

1. I like to eat **Chinese** food. (China)

2. Is the hot dog an **American** invention? (America)

3. **Siberian** tigers are endangered. (Siberia)

4. Do you like **Japanese** green tea? (Japan)

5. Homer was a famous **Greek** poet. (Greece)

6. Curry is a tasty **Indian** spice. (India)

7. St. Petersburg is a major **Russian** city. (Russia)

8. A **Swiss** skier won the downhill race. (Switzerland)

9. They danced for hours to **Brazilian** music. (Brazil)

10. At one time there were twenty-one **Spanish** missions in California. (Spain)

11. Have you ever tasted **French** chocolate? (France)

12. The **British** flag is red, white, and blue. (Britain)

CHAPTER 4

What Makes a Good How-to Article?

• Circle the statement that is true for each pair.

1. (A) A how-to article gives the reader a set of directions.
   B. A how-to article tells the reader a sequence of events.

2. A. Unnecessary steps help add interest to the article.
   (B) The steps of a how-to article are explained in time order.

3. (A) Each step is written as an imperative sentence.
   B. Each step is written as an exclamatory sentence.

4. A. The introduction should always be catchy and clever.
   (B) The introduction tells what the reader will learn in the article.

5. (A) The conclusion might give information to help the reader.
   B. The conclusion should be the same sentence as the introduction.

• Give three examples of kinds of how-to articles. Tell the purpose of each example.

Possible answers: a recipe that tells how to make a food dish; a set of directions that tell how to put something together or use a product; a set of instructions for playing a board game; a list of directions that tell how to get from one place to another

_____

_____

_____

CHAPTER 4 Articles

• Circle the article that correctly completes each sentence. Underline the noun each article points out.

1. (The) An) stingray is a type of fish.
2. (A (An) earthquake shook our house this morning.
3. Did you get (a) an) gift for Molly for her birthday?
4. Kristy's dessert is (a (an) orange.
5. The bronze medal in gymnastics went to (a (an) American.
6. (The) A) huge trees swayed in the wind.
7. We cleared (a) an) path through the forest.
8. Carlita found (an (the) hat she had lost.

• Write a or an before each noun.

9. __an__ anteater
10. __a__ year
11. __a__ quarter
12. __an__ earthworm
13. __a__ parachute
14. __an__ iceberg

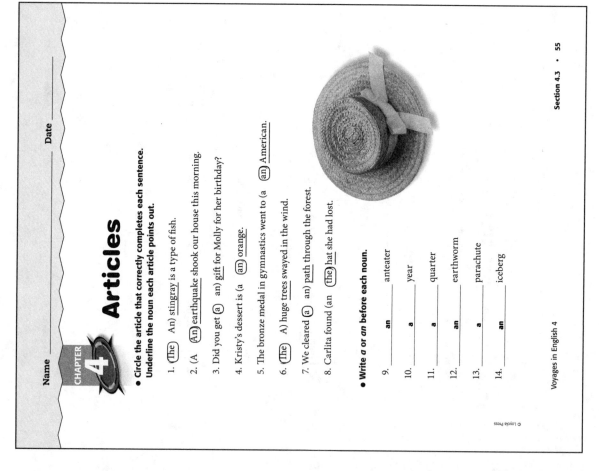

CHAPTER 4 Demonstrative Adjectives

• Underline the demonstrative adjective in each sentence. Circle the letter under the correct heading to tell whether the noun is near or far.

	Near	Far
1. How much are those running shoes?	A	(I)
2. This dessert is very good.	(N)	T
3. I think that game will be fun.	I	(A)
4. Watch out for those hornets!	T	(M)
5. These flowers are for you.	(U)	H
6. I bought these vegetables for a salad.	(S)	A
7. Open the door with this key.	(T)	C
8. That movie is really funny.	M	(E)
9. You will find the answers in these books.	(R)	S

• Now write the circled letters, in order, on the numbered lines below. If your answers are correct, you will reveal the answer to the question below.

A deer might be part of a herd, and a goose can be part of a gaggle, but where would you find a group of peacocks?

Answer:
I N A M U S T E R
1 2 3 4 5 6 7 8 9

CHAPTER 4 — Important Details

• Circle *yes* if the statement is true or *no* if it is false.

1. Make sure your directions use specific words and ideas. **(yes)** no

2. Unnecessary details make your directions easier to follow. yes **(no)**

3. If an important step is left out, your reader will still be able to follow the directions. yes **(no)**

4. In a recipe include the amount needed for each ingredient. **(yes)** no

5. In travel directions be sure to tell which way to go. **(yes)** no

6. It is not necessary to read through your steps to be sure nothing was left out. yes **(no)**

• Rewrite each direction so it includes more specific information. **Answers will vary, but students should specify:**

7. Turn at the corner of Ash and First Streets.

which direction to turn

8. Add eggs and bake for a while.

how many eggs and how many minutes to cook

9. Open the book to the correct page.

what kind of book and the exact page number

CHAPTER 4 — Adjectives That Tell How Many

• Circle the adjectives that tell how many in each sentence. The number in parentheses tells the number of words to circle in each sentence.

1. (Several) boys in the classroom have (two) pencils. (2)

2. (Ten) children went to the orchard to pick (some) apples. (2)

3. We saw (many) dolphins on a (single) boat ride. (2)

4. They found a (few) harmless snakes. (1)

5. (One) key opens the front door. (1)

6. A (dozen) eggs are in the refrigerator. (1)

7. (Various) colors were used in my painting. (1)

8. (Countless) coins lay at the bottom of the (three) pools. (2)

• Classify each circled adjective into the correct column of the chart.

Exactly How Many	About How Many
two	Several
One	few
Ten	some
dozen	Various
single	many
three	Countless

CHAPTER 4

Subject Complements

● Circle the adjective used as a subject complement in each sentence. Underline the noun it describes.

1. This story is (frightening)
2. That alarm is (loud)
3. Her friend is (nice).
4. Those cookies were (delicious)
5. Their new puppies are (playful)
6. That movie was (boring)
7. The beach was (sunny) all morning.
8. At the party many children were (noisy)

● Now find the subject complements you circled above in the word search below. The words can be horizontal, vertical, or diagonal.

```
B   R   B   F   R   I   G   H   T   E   N   I   N   G
O   S   R   I   G   H   X   C   N   I   C   E   O   P
R   C   U   D   H   E   A   L   T   H   Y   O   I   L
I   Q   U   N   I   Q   U   O   Y   S   Q   T   S   A
N   V   E   W   N   L   C   U   L   M   U   N   Y   Y
G   M   A   C   A   Y   M   D   B   Y   E   M   C   F
W   D   E   L   I   C   I   O   U   S   F   U   L   U
L   M   A   A   N   C   N   E   D   S   K   I   D   L
```

CHAPTER 4

Prefixes

● Write a word that fits each meaning. Each word should begin with the prefix dis–, pre–, or under–.

1. not connected .... **disconnected**
2. beneath one's foot .... **underfoot**
3. beneath the ground .... **underground**
4. not approved .... **disapproved**
5. pay before .... **prepay**
6. not an advantage .... **disadvantage**
7. not agree .... **disagree**
8. before the game .... **pregame**

● Use the words with prefixes you wrote to complete the sentences below.

9. The football players and fans enjoyed the **pregame** performances.
10. Their phone was **disconnected** because the bill had not been paid.
11. I have the money so we can **prepay** for parking at the airport.
12. They need shovels because the treasure is buried **underground** .
13. I felt I was at a **disadvantage** in the tennis game because of my injured wrist.
14. Mom shook her head because she **disapproved** of my new video game.
15. The puppies were **underfoot** and kept tripping me.
16. It is OK that we **disagree** because we each have our own opinion.

Adjectives That Compare

● Add –er and –est to each adjective to complete the chart.

Adjective	Compares 2 Nouns	Compares 3 or More Nouns
1. strange	stranger	strangest
2. funny	funnier	funniest
3. short	shorter	shortest
4. sad	sadder	saddest
5. long	longer	longest
6. happy	happier	happiest
7. large	larger	largest

● Use the adjectives from the chart to complete the sentences.
Use the adjectives in order. The first one is done for you.

8. Last night I had the ___strangest___ dream ever.

9. The first comic we heard was ___funnier___ than the second one.

10. December 21 is the ___shortest___ day of the year.

11. That is the ___saddest___ story I've ever heard.

12. July is a ___longer___ month than February.

13. Was Perry ___happier___ with his grade than Sue was with hers?

14. This box is ___larger___ than the one in the closet.

Irregular Adjectives That Compare

● Circle the adjective that correctly completes each sentence.

1. This was the (worst) winter we have had in years.

2. Hank is (better) best) at spelling than Lois.

3. I am bad at tennis, but my sister is even (badder (worse)).

4. What is causing that (bad worse) odor?

5. Sally's cold is (bad (worse) than Alan's.

6. Which is (gooder (better)), the strawberry or the blueberry pie?

7. My friend tells the (worse (worst)) jokes of all.

8. Is walking (better) best) exercise than jogging?

9. This is the (worse (worst)) desk in the room.

10. Beth is my (goodest (best)) friend.

11. Steve is the (best) better) musician in our band.

12. Anthony is a (good) best) baseball player.

● Write a sentence for each irregular adjective in parentheses.

13. (good) _____

14. (better) _____

15. (bad) _____

16. (worse) _____

© Loyola Press

CHAPTER 4 — Dictionary

● Write the words in alphabetical order.

1. rinse, ringlet, rival, ridicule

   ridicule, ringlet, rinse, rival

● Use the guide words from the sample dictionary page to answer the questions. Circle the letter of the answer.

$$\boxed{213 \qquad \textbf{dividend} \bullet \textbf{dollar}}$$

2. Where would you find the word *donate?*
   a. before this page   b. on this page   (c.) after this page

3. Where would you find the word *document?*
   a. before this page   (b.) on this page   c. after this page

4. Where would you find the word *diverse?*
   (a.) before this page   b. on this page   c. after this page

● Use the sample dictionary entry to determine the meaning of the word in each sentence. Circle the letter of the answer.

force (fôrs) *n.* **1** strength, power. *The explosion's force broke the window.* **2** a push or pull that changes an object's speed or direction. *The force of gravity keeps us on earth.* *v.* **3** to make do something. *The storm forced me to stay home.* **4** to break or pry open by using force. *I had to force open the window.*

5. The force of the falling tree crushed the fence.
   (a.) definition 1   b. definition 3   c. definition 4

6. The large truck almost forced our car off the road.
   a. definition 2   (b.) definition 3   c. definition 4

CHAPTER 4 — More, Most

● For each set of sentences circle the adjective in the first sentence. Then rewrite this adjective with *more* or *most* to complete the other two sentences.

1. a. The (playful) kitten batted at the yarn.
   b. This puppy is __more playful__ than the black one.
   c. Tony's parrot is the __most playful__ pet I have ever seen.

2. a. We watched the (beautiful) sunset.
   b. The peacock has the __most beautiful__ feathers of all birds.
   c. I think tulips are __more beautiful__ than roses.

3. a. Raccoons are (intelligent) mammals.
   b. Dolphins are __more intelligent__ than sharks.
   c. Some scientists think the whale is the __most intelligent__ animal.

4. a. Kangaroos have (powerful) legs.
   b. The ostrich has the __most powerful__ kick of any bird.
   c. A lizard has __more powerful__ jaws than a snake.

5. a. The model was (difficult) to build.
   b. I think spelling is __more difficult__ than math.
   c. This is the __most difficult__ test I have ever taken.

Less, Least and Fewer, Fewest

● Complete the chart. Write *Count* or *Noncount* to identify each noun. Then write the noun with each comparative form. The first one is done for you.

Noun	Count or Noncount?	Fewer or Less?	Fewest or Least?
1. leaf	Count	fewer leaves	fewest leaves
2. place	Count	fewer places	fewest places
3. peace	Noncount	less peace	least peace
4. trail	Count	fewer trails	fewest trails
5. rain	Noncount	less rain	least rain
6. freedom	Noncount	less freedom	least freedom

● Write four sentences that compare using each of the following adjectives correctly: *fewer, fewest, less,* and *least.* You may use the nouns from the chart above.

7. Answers will vary, but students should use *fewer* and *fewest* with plural count nouns and *less* and *least* with noncount nouns.

8. _____

9. _____

10. _____

Time Words

● Number these steps to show the correct order.

1. **3**   Spread the tuna mixture onto two slices of bread.

2. **2**   Mix the tuna and three tablespoons of mayonnaise in a bowl.

3. **4**   Top the tuna mixture with a lettuce leaf.

4. **5**   Cut the sandwich in half and enjoy.

5. **1**   Open a can of tuna and drain off the water.

● Complete the instructions below using the ordered sentences from above. Add time words to help connect the ideas.

To make a tuna fish sandwich you will need a can of tuna, mayonnaise, lettuce, two slices of bread, a spoon, and a knife.

Answers will vary, but students should add a time word to the beginning of each sentence.

_____

_____

_____

_____

● Copy a sequence chart onto a separate sheet of paper. Complete the chart with the steps for making a favorite snack. Add a time word to each step to make the directions easier to follow. For an example of a sequence chart see page 137.

Name _____ Date _____

CHAPTER 4

Position of Adjectives

- Circle the descriptive adjective in each sentence. Write *before* or *after* to identify the position of the adjective.

1. These pants are (long). _____ after

2. The (restless) children needed a nap. _____ before

3. (Golden) leaves floated to the ground. _____ before

4. Reptiles are (scaly) creatures. _____ before

5. The chair looked (unsteady). _____ after

6. The (popular) movie is never in stock. _____ before

7. This trail is (steep). _____ after

- Write two of your own sentences on the lines below. Write one with the adjective before the noun and one with the adjective after. Draw a picture that illustrates each sentence.

Answers will vary.	Answers will vary.

Voyages in English 4   Section 4.11 • 67

© Loyola Press

Name _____ Date _____

CHAPTER 4

Self-Assessment

- Check *Always*, *Sometimes*, or *Never* to respond to each statement.

Writing	Always	Sometimes	Never
I can identify the features of a how-to article.			
I can identify and use important details in a how-to article.			
I can identify prefixes and use them to understand the meanings of words.			
I can identify the features of a dictionary.			
I can identify and use time words.			

Grammar	Always	Sometimes	Never
I can identify and use descriptive adjectives.			
I can identify and use proper adjectives.			
I can identify and use articles.			
I can identify and use demonstrative adjectives.			
I can identify and use adjectives that tell how many.			
I can identify and use subject complements.			
I can identify and form adjectives that compare.			
I can identify and use irregular adjectives that compare.			
I can identify and use adjectives that compare with *more* and *most*.			
I can identify when to use the adjectives *less*, *least* and *fewer*, *fewest*.			
I can identify whether an adjective comes before or after a noun.			

- **Explain how learning about adjectives can make your writing more specific.**

_____

68 • Chapter 4 Self-Assessment   Voyages in English 4

© Loyola Press

Action Verbs

- Complete each sentence with an action verb from the word box. Use each verb once.

| hit | dropped | gallops | thanked | fixed |
| peeled | found | eats | swims | danced |

1. We **thanked** our friends for helping us.

2. Miguel and Laura **danced** to the music.

3. The last batter up **hit** a home run.

4. The outfielder **dropped** the ball.

5. Jim **eats** two sandwiches for lunch.

6. Jennifer **swims** across the pool six times each day.

7. The horse **gallops** around the corral.

8. Have you **found** the lost glove?

9. Mom **peeled** the potatoes and cooked them.

10. The plumber **fixed** the broken water pipe.

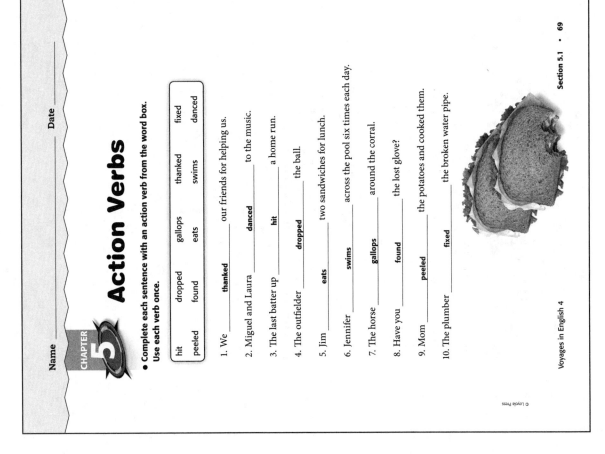

© Loyola Press

Being Verbs

- Underline the verb in each sentence. Write *action* or *being* to identify the verb. Hint: Some being verbs are formed with two words.

1. Andrew <u>will be</u> the star of the show. **being**

2. Joe and Marcie <u>have been</u> good friends since first grade. **being**

3. The black squirrel <u>gathered</u> nuts. **action**

4. I <u>am</u> the captain of our baseball team. **being**

5. Dave <u>wrote</u> a note to his teacher. **action**

6. It <u>has been</u> a very hot summer. **being**

7. A rattlesnake <u>is</u> a reptile. **being**

8. The Luzon brothers both <u>play</u> the piano. **action**

- Write a being verb to complete each sentence.

9. Yesterday the children **were** noisy.

10. Neptune and Venus **are** planets.

11. Andrew Jackson and Theodore Roosevelt **were or have been** U.S. presidents.

12. Today Ted **is or will be** our waiter.

© Loyola Press

Practice Book Answers • **39**

CHAPTER 5

What Makes Good Persuasive Writing?

• Find the phrase in the right column that completes each statement in the left column. Write the letter of the phrase on the line.

1. The purpose of persuasive writing is to **c** .

2. When you state your position, **a** .

3. You should give reasons because **e** .

4. When you include an example, **d** .

5. Think about your audience and **b** .

a. you tell how you feel about a particular topic

b. use reasons and language that appeal to them

c. convince readers to think or act in a certain way

d. it helps readers see how your reasons support your position

e. they help persuade others to agree with you

• Think about a vacation that you would like to persuade your family to take. Complete the following parts of a persuasive piece.

6. State your position: _____   **Answers will vary.**

7. Give three reasons that support your position: _____

_____

_____

8. Give two examples that support your position: _____

_____

CHAPTER 5

Linking Verbs

• Underline the linking verb in each sentence. It can be one or two words. Circle the subject complement. Then circle the correct letter to tell if the subject complement is a noun, a pronoun, or an adjective.

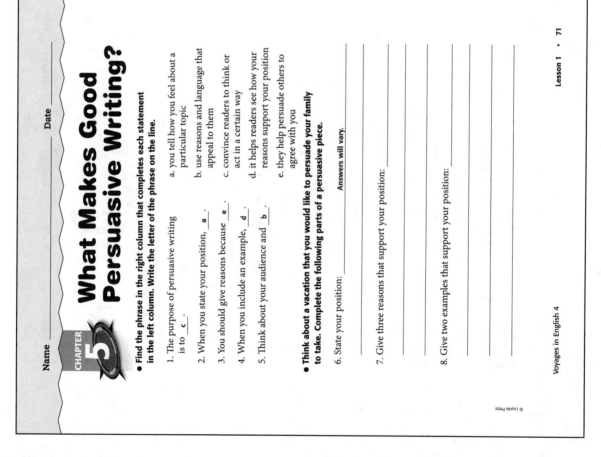

	Noun	Pronoun	Adjective
1. Thomas Edison was an (inventor)	(F)	S	K
2. This orange juice is (sweet)	T	I	(O)
3. The tallest student in our class is (he)	A	(O)	T
4. That man will be the next (mayor)	(T)	M	C
5. The Medinas are good (neighbors)	(S)	H	P
6. They are (quiet)	E	B	(T)
7. The next person in line is (she)	O	(E)	N
8. Rosanna has been (friendly)	U	O	(P)
9. I am an avid (fan) of hockey.	(S)	P	K

• Now write the circled letters, in order, on the numbered lines. If your answers are correct, you will reveal the answer to the riddle.

The more of these you take, the more you leave behind. What are they?

Answer:

F	O	O	T	S	T	E	P	S
1	2	3	4	5	6	7	8	9

CHAPTER 5

Helping Verbs

● Write a helping verb to complete each sentence. There is more than one right answer for each item. Then go back and circle the main verb in each sentence.   *Possible answers:

1. Jackson ____ **is*** (eating) his dessert.

2. We ____ **will*** (sail) from Portland to Bailey Island next year.

3. My aunt Mary ____ **has*** (planned) a trip to Mexico.

4. Yesterday we ____ **were*** (swimming) for over an hour.

5. Next year they ____ **will*** (move) to another state.

6. Jeremy ____ **should*** (help) you with your homework.

7. Ellen and Richard ____ **will*** (lead) the parade.

8. Manual ____ **must*** (finish) his homework before dinner.

9. We ____ **are*** (weaving) baskets at camp.

10. Todd and Emily ____ **should*** (visit) their grandmother.

11. The refrigerator ____ **is*** (making) a strange noise.

12. Tom ____ **can*** (walk) home from school.

● Write three sentences of your own. Use each verb in parentheses as a helping verb.

13. (can) _____

14. (have) _____

15. (am) _____

CHAPTER 5

Fact and Opinion

● Write *fact* or *opinion* to identify each sentence. Below each write a sentence to explain why you chose your answer.
Sample answers:

1. Students waste their after-school time playing video games. **opinion**

   Not everyone may think the time is wasted.

2. The new math computer game costs $29.95. **fact**

   This information can be checked.

3. Highway 50 runs from California through Nevada. **fact**

   This could be checked on a map.

4. Mr. Wilson is the principal of Oakville Elementary School. **fact**

   This could be checked by calling the school.

5. Mr. Wilson is the most popular principal the school has had. **opinion**

   This cannot be checked; not everyone may agree with this.

6. Football is an exciting sport. **opinion**

   This cannot be checked; not everyone thinks football is exciting.

● Copy a blank fact-and-opinion chart onto a separate sheet of paper. Choose a topic you have recently studied in social studies or science. Complete the chart by writing three facts and three opinions about this topic. Discuss with a partner what makes each statement a fact or an opinion. For an example of a fact-and-opinion chart see page 138. Answers will vary.

Practice Book Answers • **41**

CHAPTER 5

Principal Verb Parts

• **Write the form of the verb in parentheses to complete each sentence.**

1. Mark has **called** his friend for help with the assignment. (call—past participle)

2. Pedro **slammed** the door when he came into the house. (slam—past)

3. My grandmother is **baking** a blackberry pie. (bake—present participle)

4. Who **asked** for a piece of cake? (ask—past)

5. Jim had **frosted** the cake, and his fingers were sticky. (frost—past participle)

6. Jun **practices** the guitar every day. (practice—present)

7. My brother is **waiting** for the mail to arrive. (wait—present participle)

8. We have **watched** the movie three times. (watch—past participle)

9. The soccer team **played** two games yesterday. (play—past)

10. The puppy **chewed** on my new shoe. (chew—past)

11. Tyrone **likes** peppers on his hot dog. (like—present)

12. I have **circled** the pages to review for the test. (circle—past participle)

CHAPTER 5

Verb Phrases

• **Underline the verb phrase in each sentence. Circle the main verb.**

1. They are (writing) letters to their senator.
2. Pam could (win) the relay race.
3. It will (rain) this afternoon.
4. I should have (finished) my homework by now.
5. The team must be (practicing) now.
6. Rashad can (play) the drums.

• **Write a helping verb to complete the verb phrase in each sentence. There is more than one right answer for each item.**
Possible answers:

7. The cat **was or is** playing with the yarn.

8. You **could, should, or may** have written the letters already.

9. The train **could, will, should, or may** travel up the mountain.

10. They **are or were** swimming in the pond.

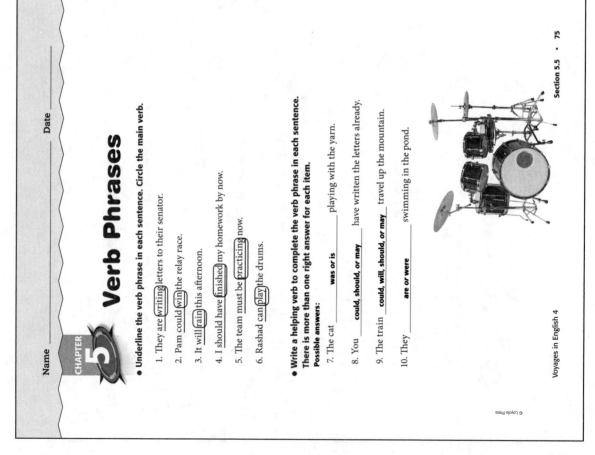

Name _____ Date _____

Irregular Verbs

- Write the present or present participle form of the verb in parentheses to complete each sentence.

1. Big waves are **breaking** (break) against the shore.

2. The students in our class **know** (know) how to do algebra problems.

3. The clay in the sculptures we made is **beginning** (begin) to harden.

4. Sheldon sometimes **breaks** (break) dishes when he is drying them.

5. Our after-school computer class **begins** (begin) at 3:15.

6. Mimi **knows** (know) the last line of the poem.

- Write the past or past participle form of the verb in parentheses to complete each sentence.

7. I **broke** (break) the piñata at the party, and a lot of candy fell out.

8. Kaitlin has **known** (know) her best friend, Luisa, since preschool.

9. I have **begun** (begin) piano lessons.

10. My friend has **broken** (break) his promise to help me with my project.

11. I **knew** (know) how to solve the final problem on the test.

12. The choir **began** (begin) the concert 15 minutes late.

Name _____ Date _____

Synonyms

- Write a synonym for each word.
Sample answers:
1. quickly **fast, rapidly**
2. wrong **incorrect**
3. genuine **real**
4. sleepy **tired**
5. small **tiny, little**
6. quarrel **argument, fight**

- Use the synonym pairs from above to complete the sentences. Check that the synonyms you choose make sense in the sentence.
Sample answers:

7. A flea is **small** in size, and a mite is **little** too.

8. We took a(n) **wrong** turn because our directions were **incorrect**.

9. A horse runs **quickly**, but a jaguar also moves **fast**.

10. The vase was a(n) **genuine** antique, but the coin was not **real** gold.

11. I was **sleepy** from reading so long, but Jay was **tired** because he stayed up too late.

12. The **quarrel** between Ana and Sofia was a(n) **argument** about who should clean up the mess.

CHAPTER 5 — More Irregular Verbs

● **Circle the correct verb form to complete each sentence.**

1. I am (chose (choosing)) a new topic for my project.

2. She (doing (did)) me a favor today.

3. Grandmother ((taught) teached) me how to knit last year.

4. Have you ((done) did) your report yet?

5. ((Choose) Chose) a book or a video you want to use.

6. Brian (do (does)) his chores eagerly.

7. I am (teach (teaching)) my sister how to ride a skateboard.

8. Mr. Payson has (teaching (taught)) me how to play the piano.

● **Write a sentence that includes the form of the verb in parentheses. Answers will vary, but students should use these verb forms:**

9. choose (past participle) _____ **chosen**

10. do (present participle) _____ **doing**

11. teach (present) _____ **teach or teaches**

12. choose (past) _____ **chose**

CHAPTER 5 — Dictionary

● **Find each word in the dictionary. Rewrite the word, adding a dot to separate the breaks as they appear in the entry.**

1. carnivorous _____ **car·niv·o·rous**

2. articulate _____ **ar·tic·u·late**

3. pediatrician _____ **pe·di·a·tri·cian**

4. generosity _____ **gen·er·os·i·ty**

5. irresistible _____ **ir·re·sis·ti·ble or ir·re·sist·i·ble**

6. sumptuous _____ **sump·tu·ous**

● **Find each word in the dictionary. Write the respelling of the word as it appears in the entry.**

7. hideous _____ **hĭd′e·as**

9. knight _____ **nīt**

8. zucchini _____ **zōō – kē′ nē**

10. chaotic _____ **kā – ŏt′ĭk**

● **Find each word in the dictionary. Rewrite the word, adding a dot to separate the syllables. Then circle the most heavily accented syllable.**

11. pedigree _____ **(pedi)·gree**

12. possess _____ **pos·(sess)**

13. flamingo _____ **fla·(min)·go**

14. disapprove _____ **dis·ap·(prove)**

CHAPTER 5 — Simple Present Tense

• Use the correct verb from the word box to complete each sentence.

close	laugh	feed	serve	ride	write
closes	laughs	feeds	serves	rides	writes

1. That store **closes** at five o'clock.

2. Henry **feeds** his cat twice a day.

3. Each month the students **write** to their pen pals in Japan.

4. The campers **ride** horses to the campsite.

5. On Sundays, my mother **serves** spinach for dinner.

6. Ralph always **laughs** at my jokes.

7. The waiters **serve** the guests at weddings.

8. Tyesha **writes** stories about a magical kingdom.

9. Every summer Elena **rides** the roller coaster a dozen times.

10. We **laugh** every time he tells that funny story.

11. The supermarkets **close** on Thanksgiving Day.

12. The children **feed** the chickens scraps after dinner.

Voyages in English 4   Section 5.9 • 81

CHAPTER 5 — Simple Past Tense

• Write the correct simple past tense form of the verb in parentheses to complete each sentence.

1. (drink) Tim **drank** all of the milk last night.

2. (visit) We **visited** my grandfather in Florida.

3. (enjoy) Freddy and Mark **enjoyed** the concert very much.

4. (study) We **studied** hard for our math test.

5. (wrap) Mom and Dad **wrapped** all the presents themselves.

6. (try) I **tried** to find my missing notebook.

7. (give) My parents **gave** two new books to the library.

8. (slide) The otters **slid** into the river.

• Write four sentences about something you did with your family last weekend. Use four simple past tense verbs.

Answers will vary.

9. _____

10. _____

11. _____

12. _____

82 • Section 5.10   Voyages in English 4

CHAPTER 5

Future Tenses

- **Rewrite each sentence in the future tense, using *will*.**

1. The magician performs every Friday.

   The magician will perform every Friday.

2. Who does the dishes after supper?

   Who will do the dishes after supper?

3. Each person brings some food to the picnic.

   Each person will bring some food to the picnic.

4. The archer shoots an arrow at the target.

   The archer will shoot an arrow at the target.

- **Rewrite each sentence in the future tense, using *going to*.**

5. The puppy chews on the bones.

   The puppy is going to chew on the bones.

6. Ted and Laura send their aunt a letter.

   Ted and Laura are going to send their aunt a letter.

7. I play baseball in the summer.

   I am going to play baseball in the summer.

8. The actors perform on an outdoor stage.

   The actors are going to perform on an outdoor stage.

CHAPTER 5

Compound Subjects and Predicates

- **Rewrite each pair of sentences with a compound subject.**
  Possible answers:

1. Sammy won a prize. Janet also won a prize.

   Sammy and Janet won prizes.

2. The clock is broken. The radio is broken too.

   The clock and the radio are broken.

3. Has the cat been fed? Has the dog been fed?

   Have the cat and the dog been fed?

4. Jerry may win the contest. Jim may win the contest.

   Jerry or Jim may win the contest.

- **Rewrite each pair of sentences with a compound predicate.**
  Possible answers:

5. Enrique might go to the park. He might walk his dog instead.

   Enrique might go to the park or walk his dog.

6. The cat ate its dinner. It fell asleep by the fire.

   The cat ate its dinner and fell asleep by the fire.

7. I worked hard. I did not finish on time.

   I worked hard but did not finish on time.

8. Dad will drive you to practice. He will pick you up at 6:00.

   Dad will drive you to practice and pick you up at 6:00.

Chapter 6 — Progressive Tenses

Name _____ Date _____

CHAPTER 6

Progressive Tenses

- Underline the present progressive verb in each sentence. Rewrite the sentence using the past progressive form of the verb. Hint: The verb is made up of two words.

1. Anthony is reading a book about Lewis and Clark.

   Anthony was reading a book about Lewis and Clark.

2. I am preparing for my test.

   I was preparing for my test.

3. Jim and Terry are laughing at the silly joke.

   Jim and Terry were laughing at the silly joke.

4. The trees in our yard are losing their leaves.

   The trees in our yard were losing their leaves.

5. Mr. Johnson is traveling across the country.

   Mr. Johnson was traveling across the country.

6. I am typing my letter on a computer.

   I was typing my letter on a computer.

7. They are filing papers in the file cabinet.

   They were filing papers in the file cabinet.

8. She is driving to the grocery store.

   She was driving to the grocery store.

Chapter 5 — Self-Assessment

Name _____ Date _____

CHAPTER 5

Self-Assessment

- Check *Always, Sometimes,* or *Never* to respond to each statement.

Writing	Always	Sometimes	Never
I can identify persuasive writing and its features.			
I can identify facts and opinions.			
I can identify and use synonyms.			
I can identify and use the features of a dictionary.			
I can identify compound subjects and predicates and use them correctly in my writing.			

Grammar	Always	Sometimes	Never
I can identify and use action and being verbs.			
I can use identify and use linking verbs.			
I can identify and use helping verbs.			
I can identify and use verb phrases.			
I can identify principal parts of verbs and use them correctly.			
I can identify the irregular verbs *begin, break,* and *know* and use them correctly.			
I can identify the irregular verbs *choose, do,* and *teach* and use them correctly.			
I can identify simple present tense verbs and use them correctly.			
I can identify simple past tense verbs and use them correctly.			
I can identify future tense verb forms that use *will* and *going to* and use them correctly.			

- **Explain how using different verb forms can make your writing more precise.**

CHAPTER 6

Present Perfect Tense

• Use the verb in parentheses in the present perfect tense to complete each sentence.

1. Elena **has read** this book before. (read)

2. My parents **have worked** hard on the yard all day. (work)

3. You **have remembered** to bring your bathing suit. (remember)

4. My older brother **has driven** across country. (drive)

5. We already **have practiced** many hours for the band concert next week. (practice)

6. The child **has broken** the new vase. (break)

7. We **have cleaned** the house for the party. (clean)

8. I **have flown** in an airplane several times. (fly)

9. The flower in the vase **has wilted** . (wilt)

10. Mr. Thompson **has bought** a new car. (buy)

• Write about things you and your classmates have done this year. Include four verbs in the present perfect tense.

Answers will vary.

_____

_____

_____

_____

CHAPTER 6

What Makes a Good Fable?

• Circle the letter of the answer that best completes each statement.

1. An appropriate setting for a fable about a rabbit and a coyote would be a _____.

   a. rain forest in Brazil   (b.) desert in Mexico   c. park in a big city

2. _____ might be characters in a fable about two enemies that learn the importance of friendship.

   (a.) A python and a mongoose   b. The sun and the moon   c. A boy and a girl

3. _____ might be characters in a fable with Australia's Great Barrier Reef as the setting.

   a. A kangaroo and a koala   b. A rattlesnake and a mouse   (c.) A shark and an octopus

4. A problem that could be resolved in a fable is _____.

   (a.) how the forest animals learn to love a skunk despite its smell
   b. how the colors of a rainbow came to be in the sky
   c. how humans kept from sailing off the edge of the earth

5. The following would be a good moral for a fable: _____.

   a. There are ten steps to building a go-cart.
   (b.) The help of a friend can save you time.
   c. This was an adventure I'll never forget.

• Look at the sample story map on page 137. Copy a blank story map onto a separate sheet of paper. Describe characters, a setting, and events that you could write about in a fable. Use your completed story map to write a fable on a separate sheet of paper.
Answers will vary.

Chapter 6 — Past Perfect Tense

Name _____ Date _____

CHAPTER 6

Past Perfect Tense

• Write the past perfect tense of each verb in parentheses. Remember that some verbs are irregular and have irregular past participles.

1. I **had torn** (tear)
2. He **had finished** (finish)
3. They **had walked** (walk)
4. It **had rattled** (rattle)
5. She **had picked** (pick)
6. You **had written** (write)
7. We **had drawn** (draw)
8. I **had broken** (break)

• Use the past perfect verbs you wrote to complete these sentences.

9. The woman **had written** the letter before she got the phone call.
10. The children **had walked** home before it started to rain.
11. Vincent **had finished** his homework before he went out to play.
12. Aunt Margie **had picked** fresh tomatoes before she made the sauce.
13. After the street artist **had drawn** my portrait, she let me see it.
14. After the loose window **had rattled** all night, my brother fixed it.
15. After the hem **had torn**, I stitched it.
16. The car **had broken** down three times before we sold it.

Voyages in English 4   Section 5.14 • 89

Chapter 6 — Future Perfect Tense

Name _____ Date _____

CHAPTER 6

Future Perfect Tense

• Write the future perfect tense of each verb in parentheses.

1. He **will have studied** (study)
2. She **will have returned** (return)
3. We **will have left** (leave)
4. It **will have cooked** (cook)
5. We **will have visited** (visit)
6. I **will have saved** (save)
7. She **will have spent** (spend)
8. He **will have waited** (wait)

• Use the future perfect verbs you wrote to complete these sentences.

9. I **will have saved** over a hundred dollars by my birthday.
10. This amusement park is so expensive that she **will have spent** all of her money by evening.
11. We **will have left** the party by the time you arrive.
12. Sam **will have studied** for several days before he takes the test.
13. Before you get home from school, Mom **will have returned** from the store.
14. The turkey **will have cooked** for five hours by dinnertime.
15. By the time this bus arrives, Sarah **will have waited** for fifteen minutes.
16. Once summer ends, we **will have visited** the beach five times.

90 • Section 5.15   Voyages in English 4

© Loyola Press

CHAPTER 6 — Beginning, Middle, and Ending

Name _____ Date _____

• Read each statement about fables. Write *yes* if the statement is true or *no* if it is false. If the statement is false, rewrite it to be true.

1. Describe the setting or characters at the end of a fable.   **no**

   A fable should describe the setting and characters at the beginning.*

2. The problem the characters face should be introduced at
   the beginning.   **yes**

3. The problem is solved at the end of the fable, and it is always
   a happy ending.   **no**

   The problem is solved at the end, but the ending may not be happy.*

4. The middle of the fable teaches a lesson.   **no**

   The end of the fable teaches a lesson.*

5. Sometimes the main character learns a lesson the hard
   way in the ending.   **yes**

6. In the ending the author hints at the moral of a fable but
   never states it.   **no**

   In the ending the author often states the moral of the fable.*

7. The middle of a fable gives the details needed to tell
   the story.   **yes**

*Possible answers

Voyages in English 4   Lesson 2 • 91

© Loyola Press

CHAPTER 6 — Subject-Verb Agreement

Name _____ Date _____

• Circle the verb that agrees with the subject to complete each sentence.

1. They (was (were)) writing letters to their senator.

2. Chuck ((is) are) singing in the concert next week.

3. ((Does) Do) you have the keys?

4. The boy said he (were (was)) finished with his homework.

5. I ((am) is) waiting for the mail.

6. Ed (does (does)) do) not play computer games well.

7. Our cousins (does (do)) not visit every summer.

8. They (was (were)) sailing boats in the pond.

• Write a sentence that includes each verb phrase. Make sure
subjects and verbs agree.

9. does not write:

   Answers will vary, but students should use correct subject-verb agreement.

10. do call: _____

11. am hoping: _____

12. were jumping: _____

92 • Section 5.16   Voyages in English 4

© Loyola Press

Name _____ Date _____

CHAPTER 6

Homophones

- Use the homophones in the first box to complete the sentences in the second box.

1. they're their there	a. The children are eating because **they're** ___ hungry. b. **There** ___ are six pencils under my desk. c. The students finished writing **their** ___ stories.
2. too two to	a. You can go with me **to** ___ the park. b. The child is **two** ___ years old today. c. The pan is **too** ___ hot to pick up.
3. knew new	a. My dad bought a **new** ___ car. b. Sarah thought she **knew** ___ the correct answer, but she was wrong.
4. hear here	a. People could **hear** ___ the thunder from miles away. b. Please place your finished reports **here** ___ .
5. hole whole	a. The six of us ate a **whole** ___ pizza. b. I found a **hole** ___ in the toe of my sock.
6. buy by	a. She didn't have enough money to **buy** ___ a ticket. b. Hector found a dollar over there **by** ___ the table.

- Look at the sample word-analysis chart on page 140. Copy two blank charts onto a separate sheet of paper. Complete the charts using a pair of homophones from above. **Answers will vary.**

Name _____ Date _____

CHAPTER 6

There Is and There Are

- Circle *is* or *are* to complete each sentence. Write *singular* or *plural* to identify the number of the subject.

1. There (is **are**) four cats on our street. — **plural**
2. There (**was** were) a loud knock at the door. — **singular**
3. There (is **are**) nice teachers at our school. — **plural**
4. There (**is** are) a message for you on my desk. — **singular**
5. There (**were** was) two frogs in the pond last night. — **plural**
6. There (was **were**) dirty dishes in the sink. — **plural**
7. There (is **are**) 30 days in September. — **plural**
8. There (**is** are) a musician onstage. — **singular**
9. There (**was** were) a single ticket left for the game. — **singular**
10. There (**was** were) a funny program on television last night. — **singular**
11. There (is **are**) spiders in the basement. — **plural**
12. There (is **are**) 50 states in the United States. — **plural**

- Think of a celebration you attended. Write three sentences with *There was* or *There were* about it. **Answers will vary.**

13. _____
14. _____
15. _____

CHAPTER 6

Adverbs of Manner

• Underline the adverb of manner in each sentence.

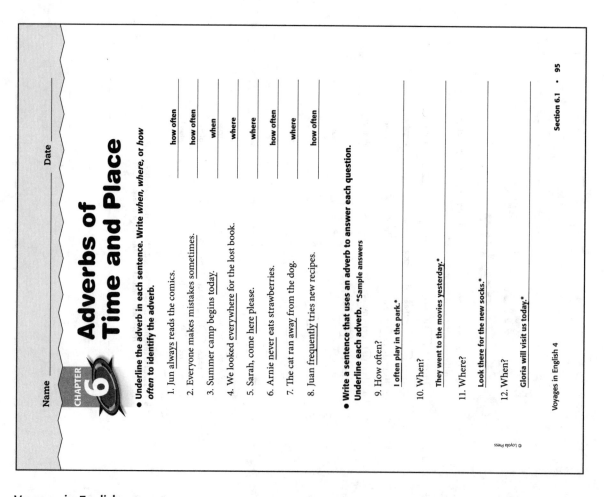

1. The tired child slept soundly.

2. The mayor eagerly shook hands with her supporters.

3. The snowflakes fell softly to the ground.

4. A good sport gracefully accepts defeat.

5. Julie gently petted the lamb.

6. The man drove slowly in the rain.

7. My uncle worked hard on the model train.

8. The children ran fast across the playground.

• Find the adverbs you underlined in the word search below.

```
O  S  O  U  N  D  L  Y  P  A  S  O  Y  H  U  S
N  S  O  M  N  P  R  H  E  R  E  S  S  A  S  L
T  Y  W  F  E  G  R  A  C  E  F  U  L  L  Y  O
F  A  S  T  S  T  R  A  N  D  Y  A  C  N  W
C  F  A  K  E  L  E  D  G  E  N  T  L  Y  S  L
E  A  G  E  R  L  Y  S  T  P  H  T  Y  B  E  Y
```

Voyages in English 4

© Loyola Press

CHAPTER 6

Adverbs of Time and Place

• Underline the adverb in each sentence. Write *when, where,* or *how often* to identify the adverb.

1. Jun always reads the comics. _____ how often

2. Everyone makes mistakes sometimes. _____ how often

3. Summer camp begins today. _____ when

4. We looked everywhere for the lost book. _____ where

5. Sarah, come here please. _____ where

6. Arnie never eats strawberries. _____ how often

7. The cat ran away from the dog. _____ where

8. Juan frequently tries new recipes. _____ how often

• Write a sentence that uses an adverb to answer each question. Underline each adverb. *Sample answers

9. How often?

I often play in the park.*

10. When?

They went to the movies yesterday.*

11. Where?

Look there for the new socks.*

12. When?

Gloria will visit us today.*

Voyages in English 4

© Loyola Press

52 • Voyages in English

Name _____ Date _____

Expanding Sentences

● **Rewrite each sentence, adding one adjective and one adverb to expand it.**

1. The author writes stories about animals.

Answers will vary, but students should add an adjective and an adverb to each sentence.

2. The waves splashed around Maggie.

_____

3. A wolf follows the rabbits.

_____

4. Roberta bought hamsters.

_____

5. The cook complained about the kitchen.

_____

6. A trumpet sounded.

_____

7. The dancer leaped across the stage.

_____

8. Dad whistled as he washed the car.

_____

9. Grandma watered her plants.

_____

10. We climb the stairs.

_____

Lesson 4 • 97

© Loyola Press

Name _____ Date _____

Adverbs That Compare

● **Underline the adverb that compares in each sentence.**

1. Of all the children at the ice cream parlor I finished my ice cream fastest.

2. Jessica woke up earlier than her brother.

3. The robin pulled harder than the worm did!

4. Hal arrived home later than Joe did.

5. Of all the fans Tam cheered loudest.

6. The train arrived sooner than the bus.

7. Of all the volunteers at the charity carwash Peter worked hardest.

8. I arrived earliest of all the visitors.

● **Draw a picture and write a sentence for each adverb that compares below.**

9. louder   10. slowest

Answers will vary, but students should use the given comparative adverb correctly.

Voyages in English 4

© Loyola Press

Practice Book Answers • **53**

CHAPTER 6

More Adverbs That Compare

● Circle the adverb that compares to correctly complete each sentence.

1. My new computer runs (more efficiently) most efficiently) than my old one.

2. It rains (more often) most often) than it snows.

3. Of all the children Charles paints (more skillfully (most skillfully).

4. Of all the group members Cherise worked (more carefully (most carefully).

5. Ben waited (more patiently) most patiently) than his brother.

6. The lamp shines (more brightly) most brightly) than the candle.

7. Snow falls (more frequently) most frequently) in the mountains than here.

8. Maria dances (more gracefully) most gracefully) than Elena.

9. Of all the walkers Karen walked (more briskly (most briskly).

10. The lion roared (more fiercely) most fiercely) than the tiger.

11. Of all the employees he works (more efficiently (most efficiently).

12. Of our whole family the baby sleeps (more soundly (most soundly).

● Write a sentence of your own for each adverb in parentheses. Answers will vary.

13. (most skillfully)

_____

14. (most eagerly)

_____

15. (more heavily)

_____

CHAPTER 6

Haiku

● Read the haiku. Make a mark above each syllable. Write the number of syllables at the end of each line.

Laughing with my friend ____ 5

I feel the warmth of friendship. ____ 7

Troubles melt away. ____ 5

● Read the haiku. Circle the line with the incorrect number of syllables. Rewrite the line to follow the rules of haiku.

The sun is so warm.

_____

I receive its energy.

_____

It warms my soul.

Students should rewrite the line so that it has five syllables. Sample answers: *It heats up my soul.* or *This star warms my soul.*

● Look at the sample five-senses chart on page 140. Copy a blank chart onto a separate sheet of paper. Complete the chart by listing words and phrases that describe a peaceful place you like to go. Then use your completed chart to write a haiku.

Answers will vary, but poems should include the features of a haiku.

Left worksheet

Name _____ Date _____

CHAPTER 6

Good and Well; Negatives

• **Write good or well to correctly complete each sentence.**

1. Alicia is a __good__ swimmer and diver.

2. I think Olivia plays piano very __well__ .

3. It is a __good__ day for a picnic, isn't it?

4. Roy did __well__ on the science test today.

5. Moles are good diggers, but they don't see __well__ .

6. The wrestler put up a __good__ fight.

• **Rewrite each sentence correctly.**

7. No one left no messages for you.*
   __No one left any messages for you.*__

8. The children did not have nothing to do.*
   __The children did not have anything to do.*__

9. There isn't no snow left on the ground.*
   __There isn't any snow left on the ground.*__

10. I never have no dessert after supper.*
    __I never have any dessert after supper.*__

*Possible answers

Voyages in English 4

Section 6.5 • 101

© Loyola Press

Right worksheet

Name _____ Date _____

CHAPTER 6

Self-Assessment

• **Check Always, Sometimes, or Never to respond to each statement.**

Writing	Always	Sometimes	Never
I can identify a fable and its features.			
I can identify the beginning, middle, and ending of a fable.			
I can identify and use homophones correctly.			
I can expand sentences by adding adjectives and adverbs.			
I can identify and write haiku poetry.			

Grammar	Always	Sometimes	Never
I can identify progressive verb tenses and use them correctly.			
I can identify the present perfect verb tense and use it correctly.			
I can identify the past perfect verb tense and use it correctly.			
I can identify the future perfect verb tense and use it correctly.			
I can identify and use correct subject-verb agreement.			
I can identify and use there is and there are.			
I can identify and use adverbs of time and place.			
I can identify and use adverbs of manner.			
I can identify and use adverbs that compare using –er and –est.			
I can identify and use adverbs that compare using more and most.			
I can correctly use good, well, and negative words.			

• **Explain how using different verb forms can make your writing more creative.**

_____

102 • Chapter 6 Self-Assessment

Voyages in English 4

© Loyola Press

CHAPTER 7

Coordinating Conjunctions

- Circle the coordinating conjunction in each sentence. Underline the words the conjunction joins.

1. Saturn (and) Neptune are planets.

2. This class was difficult (but) rewarding.

3. Did you buy a pen (or) a pencil?

4. The young child laughed (and) ran away.

5. Sarah (or) her brother needs to take out the trash.

6. The river is beautiful (but) dangerous.

- Complete each sentence with a coordinating conjunction.
Possible answers:

7. The fire sputtered __**and**__ crackled in the dark room.

8. Would you prefer a sandwich __**or**__ a cup of soup?

9. I was late for the announcement __**and**__ the presentation.

10. We ate scrambled eggs __**and**__ pancakes for breakfast.

11. Irene studied hard __**but**__ failed the exam.

12. Should I buy the red pants __**or**__ the blue skirt?

CHAPTER 7

End Punctuation

- Write declarative, imperative, interrogative, or exclamatory to identify each sentence.

1. That was the hardest test I have ever taken! __exclamatory__

2. Please turn down the radio. __imperative__

3. This photograph won an award at the art show. __declarative__

4. Wow, what an awesome car! __exclamatory__

5. Can you finish this project by noon? __interrogative__

6. How many eggs would you like for breakfast? __interrogative__

7. The breeze caused the candle to flicker. __declarative__

8. Color all of the triangles red. __imperative__

9. Mr. Velasquez works at our school. __declarative__

10. Put your dirty dishes in the sink. __imperative__

- Think about a hobby you have. On a separate sheet of paper write four sentences about your hobby: a statement, a question, a command, and a sentence of strong feeling. Remember to use the correct end punctuation.

Answers will vary, but students should include each of the four types of sentences and punctuate them correctly.

Name _____ Date _____

CHAPTER 7

Capital Letters

● Rewrite each sentence, adding capital letters where needed. The number in parentheses tells how many words need capital letters.

1. amy knightly lives on elm street. (4)

   Amy Knightly lives on Elm Street.

2. i met mrs. rodgers last fourth of july. (5)

   I met Mrs. Rodgers last Fourth of July.

3. daytona beach is in florida. (3)

   Daytona Beach is in Florida.

4. my brother's birthday is on tuesday, september 7. (3)

   My brother's birthday is on Tuesday, September 7.

5. juan just became a citizen of the united states. (3)

   Juan just became a citizen of the United States.

6. greg and i go to serenity lake every august. (5)

   Greg and I go to Serenity Lake every August.

7. aunt cho lives in new york city. (5)

   Aunt Cho lives in New York City.

8. john was born in australia, but he moved to canada when he was three. (3)

   John was born in Australia, but he moved to Canada when he was three.

Name _____ Date _____

CHAPTER 7

What Makes a Good Expository Article?

● Write yes if the statement is true or no if it is false. Rewrite each false statement to make it true.

Sample answers:

1. Most expository writing tells a reader both facts and opinions about a topic. _____ **no**

   Most expository writing tells a reader only facts about a topic.

2. Examples of expository writing include textbooks, fairy tales, biographies, and newspaper articles. _____ **no**

   Examples of expository writing include textbooks, biographies, and newspaper articles.

3. The introduction of an expository article often tells what the article will be about, and it might start with a catchy sentence. _____ **yes**

4. The body of an expository article often answers the questions *who, what, when, where, why,* and *how.* _____ **yes**

5. The most important details are presented at the end of an expository article. _____ **no**

   The most important details are presented at the beginning of an expository article.

6. A good idea for a conclusion might be a quotation or an interesting statement. _____ **yes**

● Look at the sample K-W-L chart on page 138. Copy a blank chart onto a separate sheet of paper. Use the chart to organize information for an expository article about a famous person. List what you already know and the questions you have in the first two columns of the chart. Do research to answer your questions and then list your findings in the third column. **Answers will vary.**

CHAPTER 7

Gathering Information

- **Use a word or phrase from the word box to complete each statement.**

detail	personal knowledge	written sources	fact
opinion	source	interview	quotation

1. Writers might use their **personal knowledge** to present a description of something they have seen.

2. A **fact** is something that can be proved true or false.

3. If a person's opinion is shown in a(n) **quotation** , then it can be included in an article.

4. Human sources are people that you **interview** for information.

5. A **detail** is a piece of information that supports the main idea of an article.

6. The place where you find a detail for an article is called a(n) **source** .

7. Words such as *I think, I believe, good,* and *bad* may show that a statement is a(n) **opinion** .

8. **Written sources** contain useful information, and examples include library books, Web sites, and articles.

CHAPTER 7

Titles of Works

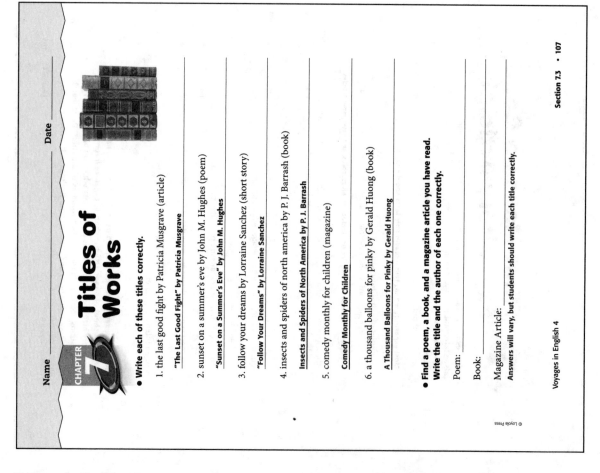

- **Write each of these titles correctly.**

1. the last good fight by Patricia Musgrave (article)

   "The Last Good Fight" by Patricia Musgrave

2. sunset on a summer's eve by John M. Hughes (poem)

   "Sunset on a Summer's Eve" by John M. Hughes

3. follow your dreams by Lorraine Sanchez (short story)

   "Follow Your Dreams" by Lorraine Sanchez

4. insects and spiders of north america by P. J. Barrash (book)

   Insects and Spiders of North America by P. J. Barrash

5. comedy monthly for children (magazine)

   Comedy Monthly for Children

6. a thousand balloons for pinky by Gerald Huong (book)

   A Thousand Balloons for Pinky by Gerald Huong

- **Find a poem, a book, and a magazine article you have read. Write the title and the author of each one correctly.**

Poem: _____

Book: _____

Magazine Article: _____

Answers will vary, but students should write each title correctly.

Name _____ **Date** _____

CHAPTER 7

Abbreviations

- Rewrite each word group, using an abbreviation for each word in italics.

1. *Sunday, February* 11

   Sun., Feb. 11

2. Fifteenth *Street*

   Fifteenth St.

3. one *inch* of ribbon

   one in. of ribbon

4. Sacramento, *California*

   Sacramento, CA

5. South River *Boulevard*

   S. River Blvd.

6. Fargo, *North Dakota*

   Fargo, ND

7. one *yard* of fabric

   one yd. of fabric

8. Houston, *Texas*

   Houston, TX

9. Raleigh, *North Carolina*

   Raleigh, NC

10. *Wednesday, April* 1

    Wed., Apr. 1

11. 1010 *North* Lassen *Avenue*

    1010 N. Lassen Ave.

12. *Thursday, December* 6

    Thurs., Dec. 6

- Find the abbreviations for the words in the word box in the puzzle.

| avenue | foot | March | September | Tuesday | Wednesday |

```
V  T  M  B  Z  M  N  P  L  X  W  B  D  A  S
L  I  A  R  T  U  E  S  H  V  E  H  V  A  T
K  O  R  V  R  H  I  Y  M  V  D  X  F  T  R
D  T  P  G  A  V  E  M  K  J  I  Y  E  Y  G
G  U  Y  W  W  S  E  I  H  K  J  S  E  P  T
```

Voyages in English 4   Section 7.4 • 109

Name _____ **Date** _____

CHAPTER 7

Personal Titles

- Rewrite each sentence, using periods and capital letters where needed.

1. mrs thompson has an appointment with dr r l lewis.

   Mrs. Thompson has an appointment with Dr. R. L. Lewis.

2. Can you give me the number for mr james m Johnson?

   Can you give me the number for Mr. James M. Johnson?

3. Sammy bought the new book by j k rowling.

   Sammy bought the new book by J. K. Rowling.

4. ms k c stone spoke at tonight's p t a meeting.

   Ms. K. C. Stone spoke at tonight's P. T. A. meeting.

5. mr and mrs sanchez hosted the party for the soccer team.

   Mr. and Mrs. Sanchez hosted the party for the soccer team.

6. His grandparents helped campaign for john f kennedy.

   His grandparents helped campaign for John F. Kennedy.

7. dr walker is her dentist.

   Dr. Walker is her dentist.

8. c s lewis is the author of my favorite book.

   C. S. Lewis is the author of my favorite book.

110 • Section 7.5   Voyages in English 4

CHAPTER 7 Negatives

• Underline the contraction with *not* in each sentence. Then write the two words that make up each contraction.

1. We won't leave until Mom gets home. — **will not**
2. The young child didn't break the vase. — **did not**
3. Jun doesn't want any more chicken. — **does not**
4. Sally can't be late, or she will not make the team. — **cannot**
5. There aren't any pencils in the box. — **are not**
6. I haven't forgotten my homework before. — **have not**

• Make each sentence more formal by removing any contractions.

7. She wouldn't have studied if I did not remind her.
   She would not have studied if I did not remind her.
8. Dad won't finish painting the garage by noon.
   Dad will not finish painting the garage by noon.
9. The children weren't playing in the sandbox.
   The children were not playing in the sandbox.
10. I couldn't understand the directions.
    I could not understand the directions.

CHAPTER 7 Commas

• Look at the comma rules below. Add commas where needed in each sentence. Then write the letter of the comma rule used in each sentence.

Comma Rules

a. before *and* or *but* to separate two parts of a compound sentence
b. to separate words in a series
c. to set off the name of the person spoken to in direct address
d. after *yes* or *no* when it introduces a sentence

1. No, I do not need a new pencil. — **d**
2. Kelly, can you help me find the meaning of this word? — **c**
3. This art project requires paper, pencils, pastels, and glue. — **b**
4. Sid needed scissors, but no one could find any. — **a**
5. Mrs. Herbert, my mom asked me to give you this note. — **c**
6. No, she did not tell me what it was about. — **d**
7. Ian, Ally, and Megan completed their mural. — **b**
8. Sir, can you tell me where the tempera paint is? — **c**
9. I looked up Monet, Picasso, and Raphael in the encyclopedia. — **b**
10. They are all artists, and this museum features their paintings. — **a**

Apostrophes (Chapter 7)

Name _____ Date _____

- Add apostrophes where needed in each sentence. Then write *possession* or *contraction* to identify how the apostrophe is used.

1. There weren't enough chairs for all the people. — contraction

2. Let's carry in more seats from the classroom. — contraction

3. They've practiced every day this week. — contraction

4. Please take these invitations to the principal's office. — possession

5. I don't have time before the bell rings for lunch. — contraction

6. Patty's costume has a tear in it. — possession

7. Have you seen Mario's hat and cane? — possession

8. The backdrop isn't finished yet. — contraction

9. We'll need to finish painting it by tomorrow. — contraction

10. Laci's mother is sitting in the front row. — possession

11. We didn't make any mistakes in the first act. — contraction

12. The people's reaction shows they liked the play. — possession

Voyages in English 4 — Section 7.7 • 113

Rambling Sentences (Chapter 7)

Name _____ Date _____

- Revise each rambling sentence to form two or three sentences.
Possible answers:

1. Two boys sat on the riverbank, and they watched the fish swim by, and they wished they had brought their fishing poles.

Two boys sat on the riverbank. They watched the fish swim by. They wished they had brought their fishing poles.

2. The man first looked to the left, and then he looked to the right, and finally he crossed the street.

The man first looked to the left. Then he looked to the right. Finally, he crossed the street.

- Revise each rambling sentence to form two sentences: one long and one short.
Possible answers:

3. I thought I had forgotten my homework, and I was worried I would get in trouble, but I found it tucked in my math book.

I thought I had forgotten my homework. I was worried I would get in trouble, but I found it tucked in my math book.

4. The squirrel ran across the top of the fence, and it chattered loudly at the cat sitting under the tree, and the cat just looked on curiously from below.

The squirrel ran across the top of the fence, and it chattered loudly at the cat sitting under the tree. The cat just looked on curiously from below.

- Revise this rambling sentence to form three sentences: one long and two short.
Possible answers:

5. The food on the table looked delicious, and Mom told us to wash our hands first, and we sat down to eat, but then Mom remembered the rolls were still in the oven.

The food on the table looked delicious. Mom told us to wash our hands first.

We sat down to eat, but then Mom remembered the rolls were still in the oven.

114 • Lesson 4 — Voyages in English 4

© Loyola Press

Name _____ Date _____

CHAPTER 7

Direct Quotations

- Add quotation marks to each sentence to identify each person's exact words.

1. Michael cried out, "Look at all the snow on the ground!"

2. "Let's go outside and play," suggested Rachel.

3. "Not before you eat breakfast," said Mom.

4. Rachel asked, "Mom, what are we having?"

5. "I think oatmeal will be good on a cold day like this," Mom replied.

6. "Oatmeal sounds good," said Michael.

- On the lines below write a short conversation between you and a friend. Use quotation marks to show the exact words each person said. Remember to include commas to separate what was said from the rest of the sentence.

Answers will vary, but students should use quotation marks and commas correctly.

_____

_____

_____

_____

_____

116 • Section 7.9

Name _____ Date _____

CHAPTER 7

Addresses

- Rewrite each set of information as an address on an envelope. Use abbreviations and capital letters where needed.

1. doctor g. h. smith, 676 hazel avenue, #3, fairview, california, 98190

```
                                          STAMP

        Dr. G. H. Smith

        676 Hazel Ave., #3

        Fairview, CA  98190
```

2. mrs trang n. nguyen, 1000 emerald bay road, boston, massachusetts, 02105

```
                                          STAMP

        Mrs. Trang N. Nguyen

        1000 Emerald Bay Rd.

        Boston, MA  02105
```

3. mister j. m. nelson, 63 twining boulevard, apartment 16, fair oaks, texas, 78754

```
                                          STAMP

        Mr. J. M. Nelson

        63 Twining Blvd., Apt. 16

        Fair Oaks, TX  78754
```

Section 7.8 • 115

© Loyola Press

CHAPTER 7 Library Catalogs

• Use the electronic catalog information to answer the questions. Use complete sentences.

El Dorado County Library Catalog
Search: Ants
Title: *Insect Engineers: The Story of Ants*
Author: Bowen, Rachel
Call No.: 595.796
Publisher: Morrow & Company: New York, NY, 2000
Summary: Describes the social structure and interactions of an ant colony.
Subjects: ants, insects, animal colonies

Possible answers:

1. What is this book about?

   It describes how ants live and interact with one another.

2. Who is the author of this book?

   Rachel Bowen is the author.

3. What is the call number for this book?

   The call number is 595.796.

4. In what year was this book published?

   It was published in 2000.

5. What other words might a person use to search for similar books on this subject?

   A person could use ants, insects, or animal colonies.

• Use your school library's card catalog or electronic catalog to look for books about one of the following topics: sports, whales, or inventions. Copy the information for one book onto an index card. On the back of the card write three questions that can be answered using the information. Trade cards with a partner and answer each other's questions. Answers will vary.

CHAPTER 7 Section 7 Review

• Rewrite each sentence, using correct punctuation and capitalization.

1. Keiko watch out for that hanging branch

   Keiko, watch out for that hanging branch!

2. The firebird is a book by jane nolan.

   The Firebird is a book by Jane Nolan.

3. Id like to buy watercolors paper and an ink pen with my money

   I'd like to buy watercolors, paper, and an ink pen with my money.

4. Tony please set lynnes book on her desk, said Ms reynolds.

   "Tony, please set Lynne's book on her desk," said Ms. Reynolds.

5. No there isnt any more milk

   No, there isn't any more milk.

6. i dont know what youre talking about said fernando.

   "I don't know what you're talking about," said Fernando.

7. have you read The golden Prize, a short story by a e schwartz

   Have you read "The Golden Prize," a short story by A. E. Schwartz?

8. dr halley lives at 16 thornhill rd apt 3.

   Dr. Halley lives at 16 Thornhill Rd., Apt. 3.

Name _____ Date _____

CHAPTER 8

Subjects, Verbs, and Direct Objects

- Diagram the sentences.

1. Peacocks eat insects.

| Peacocks | eat | insects |

2. Phil reads books.

| Phil | reads | books |

3. Horses wear saddles.

| Horses | wear | saddles |

4. Dina raises pigeons.

| Dina | raises | pigeons |

Name _____ Date _____

CHAPTER 7

Self-Assessment

- Check *Always, Sometimes,* or *Never* to respond to each statement.

Writing	Always	Sometimes	Never
I can identify an expository article and its features.			
I can find and use details for an expository article.			
I can identify and use negatives such as contractions with *not*.			
I can identify rambling sentences and rewrite them as shorter, clearer sentences.			
I can use a library card catalog and an electronic catalog to find information.			

Grammar	Always	Sometimes	Never
I can identify and use coordinating conjunctions.			
I can identify and use end punctuation.			
I can identify and use capital letters.			
I can identify and use capital letters in titles of books and poems and write the titles correctly.			
I can identify and use common abbreviations.			
I can identify and use personal titles and initials.			
I can identify and use commas.			
I can identify and use apostrophes in possessives and contractions.			
I can identify an address and write it correctly.			
I can identify and use quotation marks in direct quotations.			
I can identify when and how to use punctuation and capitalization correctly.			

- **Explain how using correct punctuation and capitalization can make your writing clearer.**

_____

CHAPTER 8

What Makes a Good Research Report?

● Circle the letter of the phrase that best completes each sentence.

1. A research report _____.
   - **a.** gives information about a topic
   - b. is an informal paper that follows no rules
   - c. is a retelling of events that have happened to you

2. The topic of a research report _____.
   - a. should be something you know nothing about
   - b. needs to be very specific and at least ten pages long
   - **c.** should interest you and the audience you are writing for

3. When researching your topic, you should _____.
   - a. use only one really good source
   - **b.** use different sources
   - c. use only information found in books

4. When you organize your information, _____.
   - **a.** group similar facts together
   - b. ignore any new questions that are raised
   - c. include both important and unimportant facts

5. The conclusion of a research report _____.
   - a. introduces new information
   - **b.** repeats the most important information
   - c. presents the writer's personal opinion about the topic

● **With a partner, choose a topic you would both like to research. Look at the sample K-W-L chart on page 138. Copy a blank chart onto a separate sheet of paper. Complete the chart by listing what you already know and what you would like to find out about the topic. Do research to answer your questions, and complete the last column of the chart.**

CHAPTER 8

Possessives and Adjectives

● Diagram the sentences.

1. Maria's team won.

2. Tired babies sleep.

3. Julio uses red ink.

4. Sandy's mother baked cookies.

CHAPTER 8

Noun Complements

• Diagram the sentences.

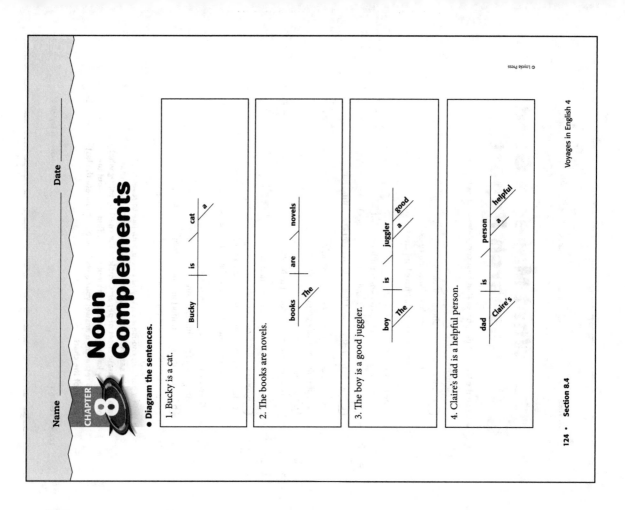

1. Bucky is a cat.

2. The books are novels.

3. The boy is a good juggler.

4. Claire's dad is a helpful person.

Voyages in English 4

CHAPTER 8

Adjective Complements

• Diagram the sentences.

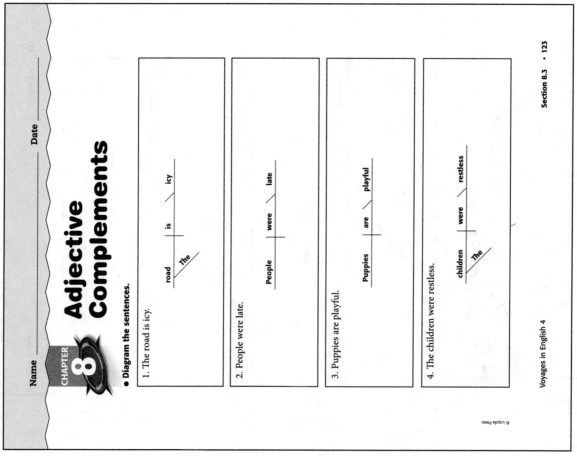

1. The road is icy.

2. People were late.

3. Puppies are playful.

4. The children were restless.

Voyages in English 4

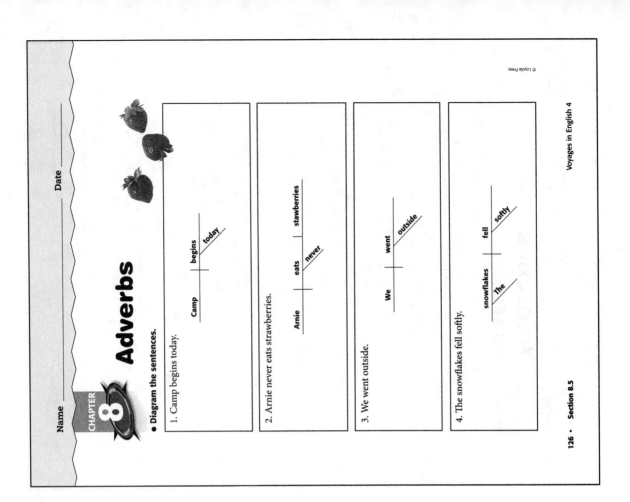

Name _____ Date _____

CHAPTER 8

Adverbs

● **Diagram the sentences.**

1. Camp begins today.

Camp | begins
 \ today

2. Arnie never eats strawberries.

Arnie | eats | stawberries
 \ never

3. We went outside.

We | went
 \ outside

4. The snowflakes fell softly.

snowflakes | fell
The \ softly

126 • Section 8.5

Voyages in English 4

© Loyola Press

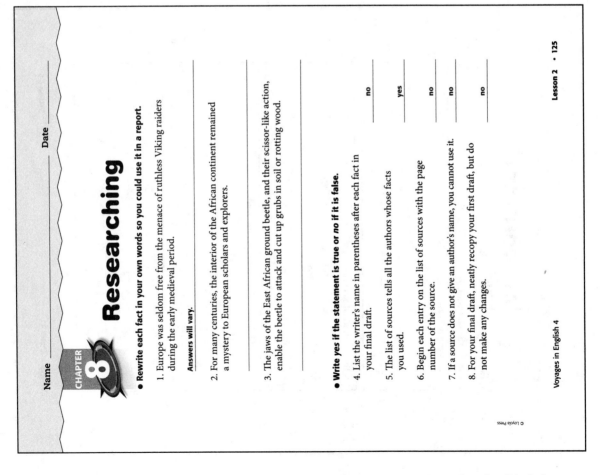

Name _____ Date _____

CHAPTER 8

Researching

● **Rewrite each fact in your own words so you could use it in a report.**

1. Europe was seldom free from the menace of ruthless Viking raiders during the early medieval period.

Answers will vary.

2. For many centuries, the interior of the African continent remained a mystery to European scholars and explorers.

3. The jaws of the East African ground beetle, and their scissor-like action, enable the beetle to attack and cut up grubs in soil or rotting wood.

● **Write yes if the statement is true or no if it is false.**

4. List the writer's name in parentheses after each fact in your final draft.   **no**

5. The list of sources tells all the authors whose facts you used.   **yes**

6. Begin each entry on the list of sources with the page number of the source.   **no**

7. If a source does not give an author's name, you cannot use it.   **no**

8. For your final draft, neatly recopy your first draft, but do not make any changes.   **no**

Voyages in English 4

Lesson 2 • 125

© Loyola Press

Practice Book Answers • 67

Page 128 — Reference Sources

Name _____ Date _____

CHAPTER 8

Reference Sources

• Match a source from the word box to each statement. Write the source on the line. You will use one source twice.

library	encyclopedia	almanac	atlas
Internet	search engine	Web sites	

1. __encyclopedia__ This is a reference source that contains general information about a topic. Topics are listed in alphabetical order.

2. __library__ This contains many books full of facts as well as reference materials. People are available to help you locate information at this place.

3. __atlas__ This contains maps that show geographical features, political features, climates, and populations.

4. __search engine__ This helps you find information on the Internet. It uses keywords to find Web sites that may have the information you are looking for.

5. __Web sites__ Pay close attention to the three letters at the end of these on the Internet. They will help you judge the reliability of the information.

6. __almanac__ This contains very recent facts as it is published every year.

7. __Internet__ This contains a vast amount of information that is available through a computer. The information found here can be very current.

8. __Web sites__ Try to find the same information at more than one of these in order to verify that a fact is true.

128 • Lesson 3

Voyages in English 4

Page 127 — Compounds: Part I

Name _____ Date _____

CHAPTER 8

Compounds: Part I

• Diagram the sentences.

1. Cats and dogs are pets.

2. Tom pitches and catches.

3. Edward Binney and Harold Smith invented crayons.

4. Omar and Rachel sing and dance.

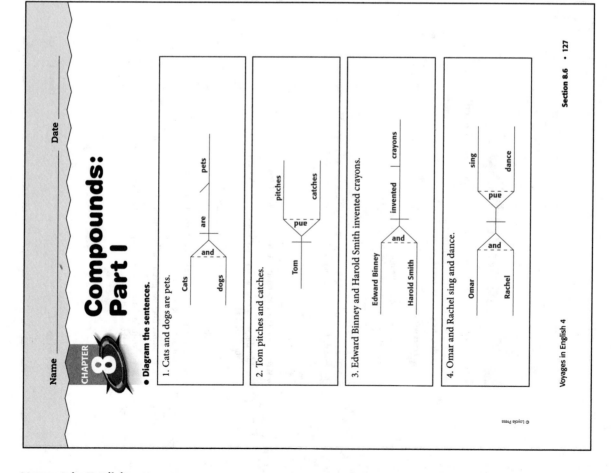

Voyages in English 4

Section 8.6 • 127

© Loyola Press

CHAPTER 8

Compounds: Part III

• Diagram the sentences.

1. Sharon's hobbies are soccer and knitting.

2. The woman is a painter and sculptor.

3. My favorite colors are blue and purple.

4. The tools are a screwdriver and a wrench.

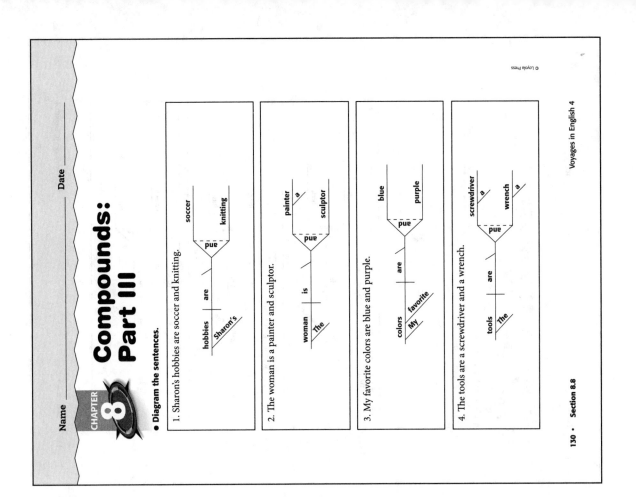

© Loyola Press

CHAPTER 8

Compounds: Part II

• Diagram the sentences.

1. Ian studies math and science.

2. Grandmother sliced cucumbers and tomatoes.

3. Mandy's horse loves apples and carrots.

4. Juan collects coins and stamps.

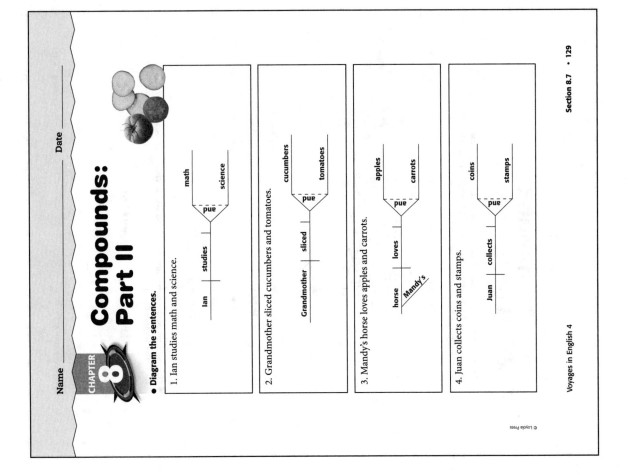

© Loyola Press

Practice Book Answers • 69

CHAPTER 8

Compound Words

• Match each word in Column A with a word in Column B to make a compound word. Write the compound words on the lines below. If you are not sure how to write the compound word, use a dictionary.

Column A   **Column B**
tooth   knob
birth   size
life   sauce
cell   maker
grown   ache
apple   phone
door   up
straw   day
trouble   berry

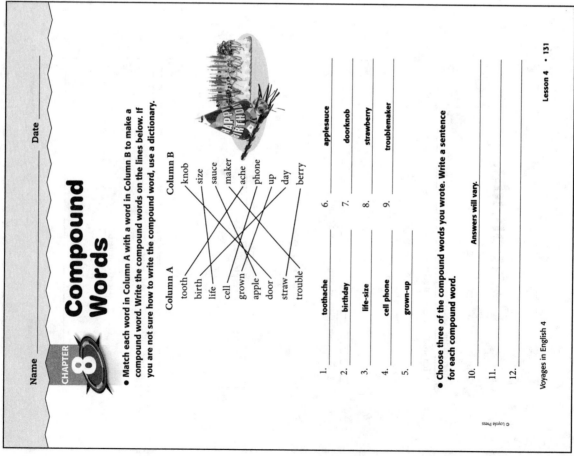

1. ____ **toothache**   6. ____ **applesauce**
2. ____ **birthday**   7. ____ **doorknob**
3. ____ **life-size**   8. ____ **strawberry**
4. ____ **cell phone**   9. ____ **troublemaker**
5. ____ **grown-up**

• Choose three of the compound words you wrote. Write a sentence for each compound word.

10. ____ **Answers will vary.**
11. ____
12. ____

CHAPTER 8

Compounds: Part IV

• Diagram the sentences.

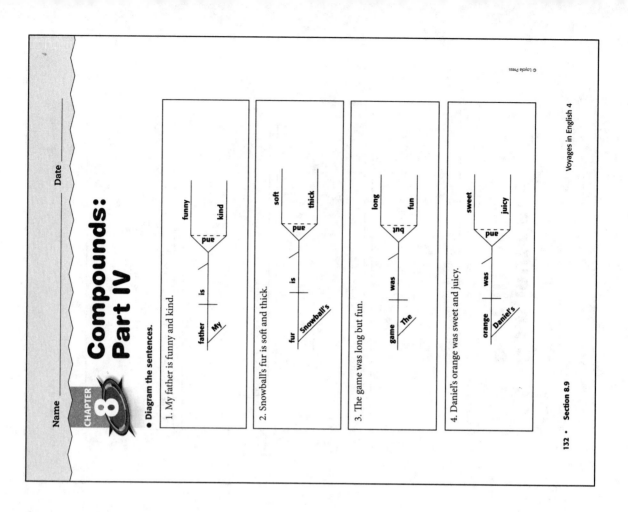

1. My father is funny and kind.

2. Snowball's fur is soft and thick.

3. The game was long but fun.

4. Daniel's orange was sweet and juicy.

CHAPTER 8

Outlines

• With a partner find sources of information about whales. Use the outline below to organize some of the information you find. For another example of an outline, see page 138.

Whales: Mammals of the Ocean
Possible answers:
I. What are the characteristics of whales?

   A. <u>Live entire life in water</u>

   B. <u>Have highly developed brains</u>

   C. <u>Are mammals</u>

II. What are the two major types of whales?

   A. <u>Baleen</u>

   B. <u>Toothed</u>

III. What is special about a whale's body?

   A. <u>Has lungs and breathes through a blowhole on top of head</u>

   B. <u>Thick layer of fat called blubber</u>

   C. <u>Broad horizontal tail flukes propel whale through water</u>

IV. How do whales get their food?

   A. <u>Some filter small prey from water</u>

   B. <u>Some work together to corral a school of fish</u>

   C. <u>Some use echolocation to find and catch prey</u>

V. How is the behavior of whales unique?

   A. <u>Some whales "sing" to each other</u>

   B. <u>Whales jump out of the water and land on their backs—an action called breaching</u>

   C. <u>Whales in pods show signs of cooperation with one another</u>

CHAPTER 8

Compound Sentences

• Diagram the sentences.

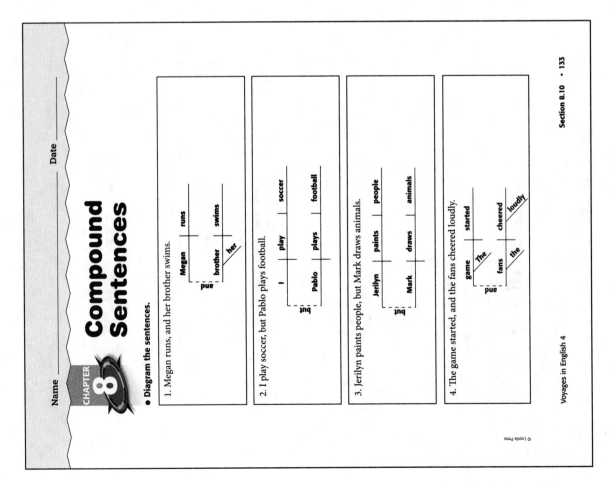

1. Megan runs, and her brother swims.

2. I play soccer, but Pablo plays football.

3. Jerilyn paints people, but Mark draws animals.

4. The game started, and the fans cheered loudly.

CHAPTER 8

Diagramming Practice

• Diagram the sentences.

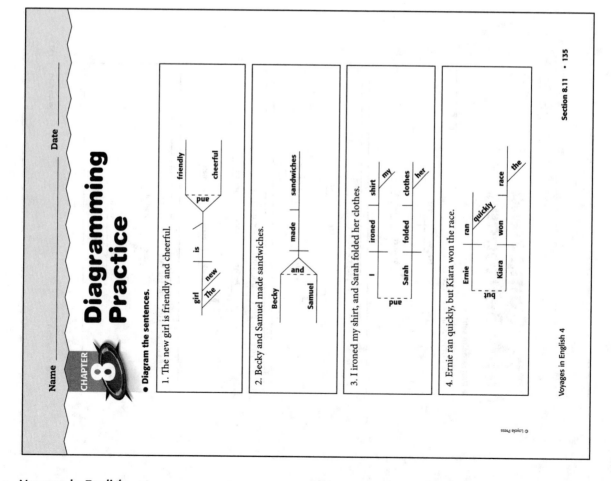

1. The new girl is friendly and cheerful.

2. Becky and Samuel made sandwiches.

3. I ironed my shirt, and Sarah folded her clothes.

4. Ernie ran quickly, but Kiara won the race.

© Loyola Press

CHAPTER 8

Self-Assessment

• Check *Always, Sometimes,* or *Never* to respond to each statement.

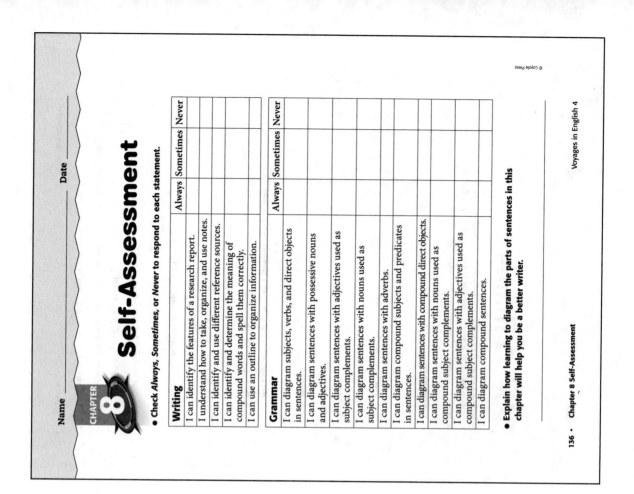

Writing	Always	Sometimes	Never
I can identify the features of a research report.			
I understand how to take, organize, and use notes.			
I can identify and use different reference sources.			
I can identify and determine the meaning of compound words and spell them correctly.			
I can use an outline to organize information.			

Grammar	Always	Sometimes	Never
I can diagram subjects, verbs, and direct objects in sentences.			
I can diagram sentences with possessive nouns and adjectives.			
I can diagram sentences with adjectives used as subject complements.			
I can diagram sentences with nouns used as subject complements.			
I can diagram sentences with adverbs.			
I can diagram compound subjects and predicates in sentences.			
I can diagram sentences with compound direct objects.			
I can diagram sentences with nouns used as compound subject complements.			
I can diagram sentences with adjectives used as compound subject complements.			
I can diagram compound sentences.			

• **Explain how learning to diagram the parts of sentences in this chapter will help you be a better writer.**

© Loyola Press

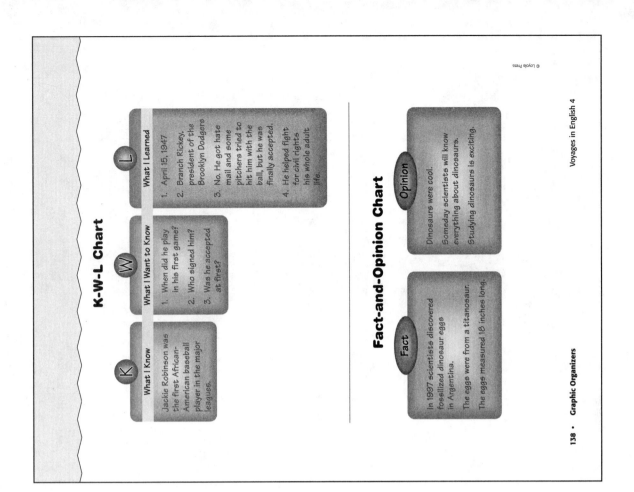

K-W-L Chart

K — What I Know
Jackie Robinson was the first African-American baseball player in the major leagues.

W — What I Want to Know
1. When did he play in his first game?
2. Who signed him?
3. Was he accepted at first?

L — What I Learned
1. April 15, 1947
2. Branch Rickey, president of the Brooklyn Dodgers
3. No. He got hate mail and some pitchers tried to hit him with the ball, but he was finally accepted.
4. He helped fight for civil rights his whole adult life.

Fact-and-Opinion Chart

Fact
In 1997 scientists discovered fossilized dinosaur eggs in Argentina.
The eggs were from a titanosaur.
The eggs measured 18 inches long.

Opinion
Dinosaurs were cool.
Someday scientists will know everything about dinosaurs.
Studying dinosaurs is exciting.

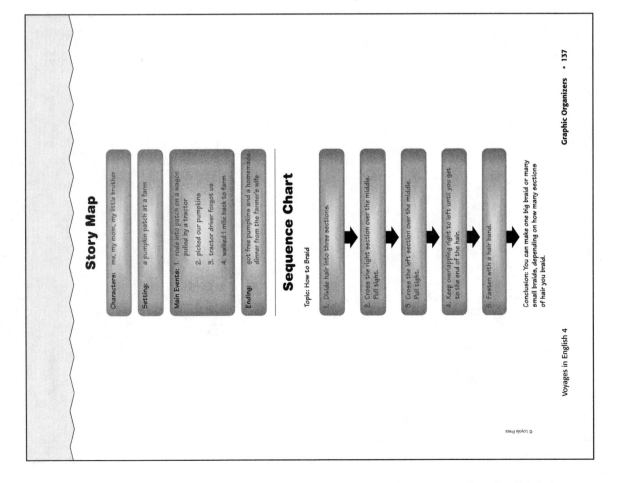

Story Map

Characters: me, my mom, my little brother

Setting: a pumpkin patch at a farm

Main Events:
1. rode into patch on a wagon pulled by a tractor
2. picked our pumpkins
3. tractor driver forgot us
4. walked 1 mile back to farm

Ending: got free pumpkins and a homemade dinner from the farmer's wife

Sequence Chart

Topic: How to Braid

1. Divide hair into three sections.
2. Cross the right section over the middle. Pull tight.
3. Cross the left section over the middle. Pull tight.
4. Keep overlapping right to left until you get to the end of the hair.
5. Fasten with a hair band.

Conclusion: You can make one big braid or many small braids, depending on how many sections of hair you braid.

Word-Analysis Chart

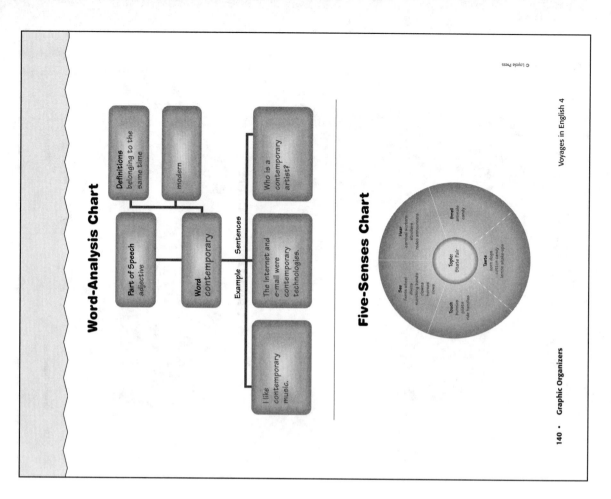

Definitions: belonging to the same time

modern

Part of Speech: adjective

Word: contemporary

Who is a contemporary artist?

The Internet and e-mail were contemporary technologies.

I like contemporary music.

Example   Sentences

Five-Senses Chart

Topic: State Fair

See: Ferris wheel, divers, microbing blanda, clowns, booths, cows

Hear: carnival workers, strollers, rodeo announcers

Smell: animals, candy

Taste: corn dogs, cotton candy, lemon shake-ups

Touch: humans, plates, ride handles

Outline

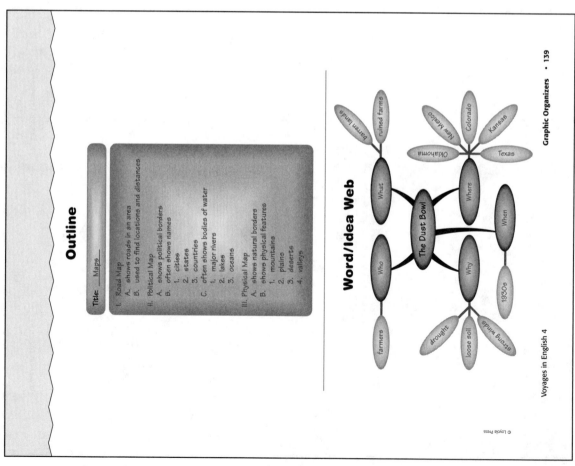

Title: Maps

I. Road Map
  A. shows roads in an area
  B. used to find locations and distances

II. Political Map
  A. shows political borders
  B. often shows names
    1. cities
    2. states
    3. countries
  C. often shows bodies of water
    1. major rivers
    2. lakes
    3. oceans

III. Physical Map
  A. shows natural borders
  B. shows physical features
    1. mountains
    2. plains
    3. deserts
    4. valleys

Word/Idea Web

The Dust Bowl

What — ruined farms, barren lands

Where — Oklahoma, New Mexico, Colorado, Kansas, Texas

When — 1930s

Why — drought, loose soil, strong winds

Who — farmers

4

Assessment Book
Answer Key

VOYAGES
IN ENGLISH
Writing and Grammar

How the Assessment Books Work

The Assessment Book provides teachers with a variety of ways to assess how their students are doing. Each chapter begins with a two-page Pre-test, for assessing students' current level of understanding, and ends with a two-page Post-test, for evaluating students' mastery of the concepts. A two-page lesson, Test Preparation, introduces students to the types of questions and subjects they will encounter on standardized tests. The Student's Genre Writing Prompt and Genre Scoring Rubric gives students the opportunity to assess their own writing skills.

Assessment Book Rubrics

Chapter Pre-tests and Post-tests (two pages each) give teachers the information they need to plan the curriculum and to assess what students have learned.

A standardized-format Genre Writing Prompt and a Student's Genre Scoring Rubric allow students to self-assess their writing skills.

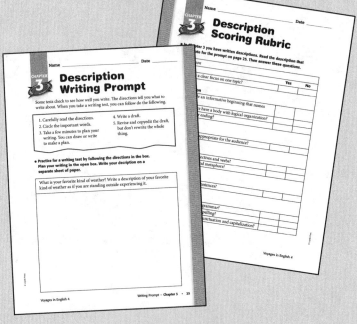

CHAPTER 1

Pre-test

Name _____ Date _____

• **Write _sentence_ or _not a sentence_ to identify each group of words.**

1. Over the prairie a very swift pony. — **not a sentence**

2. The people heard the soft melody of a flute. — **sentence**

• **Write _declarative, interrogative, imperative,_ or _exclamatory_ to identify each sentence.**

3. What pets are in the kennel? — **interrogative**

4. I have two dogs and a cat. — **declarative**

5. Do your homework before dinner. — **imperative**

• **Circle the simple subject in each sentence. Underline the simple predicate.**

6. Many (people) waved from the ship.

7. His (sister) moved to New Mexico.

• **Write _simple_ or _compound_ to identify the subject of each sentence.**

8. A squirrel and a jay fought over the seeds. — **compound**

9. Jason plays tennis on Sundays. — **simple**

• **Underline the simple predicates in each sentence. Then write _simple_ or _compound_ to identify the predicate.**

10. Our teacher plans and directs the band's concerts. — **compound**

11. My friends study and play together. — **compound**

• **Circle the subject complement in each sentence. Then write the subject that the complement tells about.**

12. The puppy is a (collie). — **puppy**

13. These people are (musicians). — **people**

• **Underline the compound predicate parts in each sentence. Then write _direct object_ or _subject complement_ to identify the use of the compound predicate parts.**

14. Mountain goats have horns and hooves. — **direct object**

15. These plants are palms and bananas. — **subject complement**

16. The fruit choices are apples and pears. — **subject complement**

• **Write _sentence_ or _run-on_ to identify each group of words.**

17. We walked down the path after the rainstorm. — **sentence**

18. I found a pencil, but I had no paper. — **sentence**

19. Mom makes soup, it is really good. — **run-on**

• **Write _yes_ if the statement is true or _no_ if it is not true.**

20. A time line helps you organize information. — **yes**

21. A time line puts events in order from left to right. — **no**

22. A time line includes events that are not important. — **no**

• **Circle the word in parentheses that is a more exact choice.**

23. Sarah (said (whispered)) "Can you give me a clue?"

24. This soup is ((delicious) good)!

25. Eager to spend my allowance, I (went (dashed)) to the store.

• **Circle the contraction with a pronoun in each sentence. Then write the two words it replaces.**

26. Mom said (you'd) help me. — **you would**

27. (He'll) take out the trash this afternoon. — **He will**

28. (We're) going to the park today. — **We are**

CHAPTER 1 Post-test

Name _____ Date _____

• **Write sentence, not a sentence, or run-on to identify each group of words.**

1. Maria played a solo at the concert. — sentence
2. I studied hard, the test was easy. — run-on
3. After the snowstorm in the evening. — not a sentence

• **Write declarative, interrogative, imperative, or exclamatory to identify each sentence.**

4. This sunset amazes me! — exclamatory
5. The young child laughed at the clown. — declarative

• **Write simple or compound to identify the subject of each sentence.**

6. Snakes and scorpions live in the desert. — compound
7. Patrick is his best friend. — simple

• **Underline the simple predicates in each sentence. Then write simple or compound to identify the predicate.**

8. The outfielder leaped and caught the ball. — compound
9. I drink milk with my sandwich. — simple

• **Draw one line under the complete subject. Draw two lines under the complete predicate.**

10. My cousin opened the cupboard.
11. Nancy plays the guitar very well.

• **Circle the direct object in each sentence.**

12. Jason opened his last (gift)
13. We placed a red (rose) in each vase.
14. Our team scored the winning (goal)

• **Circle the subject complement in each sentence. Then write noun or adjective to identify the complement's part of speech.**

15. This table is (crooked) — adjective
16. The bird in the tree is an (eagle) — noun
17. The tile was (cold) on my feet. — adjective

• **Underline the compound predicate parts in each sentence. Then write direct object or subject complement to identify the use of the compound predicate parts.**

18. The rain was cold and wet. — subject complement
19. My family eats chicken and potatoes every Sunday. — direct object
20. On our vacation we rode horses and bikes. — direct object

• **Write yes if the statement is true or no if it is not true.**

21. A time line presents ideas in time order. — yes
22. Once you make a time line, you should never change it. — no
23. Use a time line to place events in the order they happened. — yes

• **Circle the word in parentheses that is a more exact choice.**

24. The herd of buffalo (thundered / ran) up the hill.
25. Please (get / purchase) a book to read after school.
26. The insect (went / crawled) up my arm.

• **Circle the contraction with a pronoun in each sentence. Then write the two words it replaces.**

27. Harold said (he'd) be here by noon. — he would
28. (You've) been studying for two hours. — You have
29. (We're) going to the park for lunch. — We are

Right page (8)

- **Circle *Yes* or *No* for each statement.**

To be ready for tests, you should

1. skip school.   Yes   **No**
2. eat a good breakfast on the morning of the test.   **Yes**   No
3. fool around in class.   Yes   **No**
4. bring what you need.   **Yes**   No
5. pay attention.   **Yes**   No
6. never ask questions.   Yes   **No**
7. get a good night's sleep before the test.   **Yes**   No
8. forget to do your homework.   Yes   **No**

- **On the lines below write one new thing you learned about getting ready for a standardized test.**

Answers will vary.

Left page (7)

Name _____   Date _____

Getting Ready for Tests

If you are ready for a test, you will score higher. There are many things you can do to get ready for a test. Here are some things you can do every day.

- Don't miss school.
- Pay attention during every subject.
- Do all your homework.
- Read or study during some of your free time at home.

Some tests are called standardized tests. They happen every year. Standardized tests check the progress of all students in all the subjects. When you hear about this kind of test, you can

- ask questions: *What will the test look like? Will it be timed? Should I answer all the questions?*
- use your schoolbooks to review what you've learned this year.
- pay careful attention during test preparation sessions.
- get some sample test books from the library and study them with your family.

The night before a standardized test you should

- go over any sample tests one last time.
- eat a good dinner.
- get a good night's sleep.

On the day of a standardized test be sure to

- eat a good breakfast.
- get to class on time.
- bring what you need, such as a #2 pencil.

CHAPTER 1

Personal Narrative Writing Prompt

Some tests check to see how well you write. Writing tests often give you a prompt to tell you what to write about. When you take a writing test, you can do the following.

1. Carefully read the directions.
2. Circle key words.
3. Take a few minutes to plan your writing. You can draw or write to make a plan.
4. Write a draft.
5. Revise and copyedit the draft, but don't rewrite the whole thing.

- **Practice for a writing test by following the prompt in the box. Plan your writing in the open box. Write your piece on a separate sheet of paper.**

> Think of a first-time experience, such as the first time you went to the dentist or the first time you went to school. Write a personal narrative that tells about the experience.

CHAPTER 1

Personal Narrative Scoring Rubric

- **In Chapter 1 you have written personal narratives. Read the narrative that you wrote for the prompt on page 9. Then answer these questions.**

Personal Narrative

	Yes	No
Ideas		
Did I write about a real event in my life?		
Did I share my ideas in time order?		
Organization		
Does the narrative have an introduction?		
Does the narrative have a body?		
Does the narrative have a conclusion?		
Voice		
Did I write in the first-person point of view?		
Word Choice		
Did I leave out details that aren't important to the story?		
Sentence Fluency		
Did I use exact words to make my sentences interesting?		
Conventions		
Did I check for correct grammar?		
Did I check for correct spelling?		
Did I check for correct punctuation and capitalization?		

[Right page — page 12]

Circle the collective noun in each sentence.

16. The food (committee) will vote on the new rules.
17. The beekeeper removed the (swarm) of bees.
18. How many sheep are in the (herd)?

Write yes if the italicized word is a subject noun or no if it is not.

19. The rising *sun* lit up the sky.   yes
20. I saw a *fish* in the pond.   no
21. Two young *girls* jumped rope.   yes

Write yes if the compound sentence is written correctly or no if it is not.

22. The plants looked dry, I watered them.   no
23. Jenna can go to the park, or she can ride her bike.   yes
24. I had almost finished but the bell rang.   no

Write yes if the statement is true or no if it is false.

25. The return address is the address of the person
    writing the letter.   yes
26. Addresses on envelopes use abbreviations such as
    Calif. for California and *Penn.* for Pennsylvania.   no
27. The mailing address is the address of the person
    writing the letter.   no

Circle the antonym for the italicized word in each row.

28. *true*   correct   (false)   common   messy
29. *sharp*   pointy   thin   (dull)   little
30. *bent*   (straight) crooked   under   cool

[Left page — page 11]

Name _____ Date _____

CHAPTER 2 Pre-test

Underline the common noun in each sentence. Circle the proper noun.

1. My family traveled to (Tennessee).
2. (Terry) studied for his test.
3. (San Francisco) is on the coast.

Underline the singular noun in each sentence. Circle the plural noun.

4. Many dirty (dishes) are piled in the sink.
5. Two (foxes) darted across the field.
6. The child reads short (stories).

Write the plural form of the italicized noun.

7. The *child* sat quietly on the bench.   children
8. Is that *man* your uncle?   men
9. I have one loose *tooth*.   teeth

Circle the correct form of the singular possessive noun to complete each sentence.

10. This is (Brian's) Brians' project.
11. Our (family's) familys' trip begins tomorrow.
12. The (bicycle's) bicycles' front wheel is flat.

Circle the correct form of the plural possessive noun to complete each sentence.

13. Several (childs') (children's) jackets are in the closet.
14. The (babies') babie's strollers were in the hall.
15. Several (family's) (families') possessions were sold at the garage sale.

2 Post-test

● **Underline the common noun in each sentence. Circle the proper noun.**

1. (Massachusetts) is a state.

2. The (Crenshaws) own the yellow house.

3. The river rose on (Wednesday).

● **Write the plural form of each noun.**

4. ditch	**ditches**	7. ferry	**ferries**
5. goose	**geese**	8. mouse	**mice**
6. deer	**deer**	9. whistle	**whistles**

● **Rewrite each italicized phrase using a possessive noun.**

10. The *job of the man* is to clean the carpet.   **man's job**

11. Please wash the *beds of the dogs*.   **dogs' beds**

12. *Clothes for babies* are sold on the third floor.   **babies' clothes**

13. The *playground for the children* is new.   **children's playground**

● **Write *count* or *noncount* to identify the italicized noun in each sentence.**

14. I need *salt* for this recipe.   **noncount**

15. The rolling *hills* are covered by green grass.   **count**

16. I like graham crackers and *milk* as a snack.   **noncount**

17. The sound of *laughter* filled the room.   **noncount**

● **Circle the collective noun in each sentence.**

18. Every Friday our (band) plays in the park.

19. A (group) of raccoons raided the garbage cans.

● **Write *subject*, *direct object*, or *subject complement* to identify the italicized noun in each sentence.**

20. The eagle is a *predator*.   **subject complement**

21. *Biology* is the study of living things.   **subject**

22. Mrs. Thomas gave the *book* to me.   **direct object**

23. The player passed the *ball*.   **direct object**

● **Write *yes* if the compound sentence is written correctly or *no* if it is not.**

24. Shilo is my dog, Bucky is my cat.   **no**

25. The books arrived early, but the maps were late.   **yes**

26. We can have berries for dessert, or you can save them for breakfast.   **yes**

● **Write *yes* if the statement is true or *no* if it is false.**

27. The return address goes in the top right-hand corner of the envelope.   **no**

28. On an envelope the correct abbreviation to use for Kentucky is KY.   **yes**

29. The mailing address should not include any abbreviations.   **no**

● **Circle the antonym for the italicized word in each row.**

30. *happy*	silly	dull	(sad)	sour
31. *open*	empty	thin	wrong	(closed)
32. *over*	inside	crooked	(under)	off

CHAPTER 2

Multiple-Choice Tests

Some tests will ask you to choose the best answer from four answers given. These kinds of tests are called multiple-choice tests. To do the best you can on a multiple-choice test, do the following.

- Read all the directions before you begin the test.
- Read each question carefully.
- Lightly put a mark next to any answer that you know is wrong.
- If you're not sure about an answer, mark the question and move on to the next question. Come back to that question if you have time.
- Ask your teacher if it is best to guess at an answer if you're not sure, or if it is best to leave the question blank.
- Fill in the bubble on the answer sheet that matches the correct answer.

On standardized tests you are often given a Scantron sheet to record your mutiple-choice answers. When using Scantron sheets, you should do the following.

- Use only a #2 pencil to mark your answers; do not use pen or marker.
- Completely fill in each answer "bubble."
- Do not cross out any mistakes; erase them carefully.
- Do not fold or crease the Scantron sheet.

- **Fill in the sample Scantron sections to answer each question.**

1. Before taking a multiple-choice test, you should _____.

    A   eat a lot of candy   C   take a nap in class

    B   read all the directions   D   sharpen 20 pencils

    1. Ⓐ **Ⓑ** Ⓒ Ⓓ

2. When you know an answer is wrong, you should _____.

    F   raise your hand

    G   shout, "That's wrong!"

    H   fill in the matching bubble on the Scantron sheet

    J   lightly put a mark next to it

    2. Ⓕ Ⓖ Ⓗ **Ⓙ**

3. If you're not sure of an answer, you should _____.

    K   skip the question and come back to it later

    L   cry

    M   mark two bubbles on the Scantron sheet

    N   take a guess right away and forget about the question

    3. **Ⓚ** Ⓛ Ⓜ Ⓝ

4. When filling in bubbles, you should _____.

    A   use a marker   C   use a #2 pencil

    B   use a crayon   D   use a pen

    4. Ⓐ Ⓑ **Ⓒ** Ⓓ

5. When filling in bubbles, you should _____.

    F   fill in the bubble completely

    G   color outside the bubble margins

    H   make a "bubble design" on your paper

    J   leave mistakes alone without erasing them

    5. **Ⓕ** Ⓖ Ⓗ Ⓙ

CHAPTER 2

Formal Letter Scoring Rubric

• In Chapter 2 you have written formal letters. **Read the letter that you wrote for the prompt on page 17. Then answer these questions.**

Formal Letter	Yes	No
Ideas		
Did I include a clear complaint and an idea for resolution?		
Organization		
Did I use correct formal-letter format?		
Is my purpose clearly stated in the introduction?		
Does the body recount events, names, times, or dates?		
Does the conclusion sum up the information?		
Voice		
Did I use a professional, polite tone?		
Did I use formal language?		
Word Choice		
Did I use a variety of words, such as antonyms?		
Sentence Fluency		
Did I use a variety of different sentences, including compound sentences?		
Conventions		
Did I check for correct grammar?		
Did I check for correct spelling?		
Did I check for correct punctuation and capitalization?		

CHAPTER 2

Formal Letter Writing Prompt

Some tests check to see how well you write. The directions tell you what to write about. When you take a writing test, you can do the following.

1. Carefully read the directions.
2. Circle key words.
3. Take a few minutes to plan your writing. You can draw or write to make a plan.
4. Write a draft.
5. Revise and copyedit the draft, but don't rewrite the whole thing.

• **Practice for a writing test by following the directions in the box. Plan your writing in the open box. Write your formal letter on a separate sheet of paper.**

Imagine that you received a toy or game that was broken. Write a formal letter to a company to complain about the item. You can make up the inside address and the recipient's name. Be sure to include all important information in the body of the letter.

CHAPTER 3 Pre-test

● **Circle the personal pronoun in each sentence. Write *singular* or *plural* to identify the number of the pronoun.**

1. Mrs. Amesbury helped (us) with this project. ____**plural**____

2. (They) don't know where the art supplies are. ____**plural**____

3. Joe, can (you) help Terri find the camera? ____**singular**____

4. Louise and (I) finished our homework. ____**singular**____

5. (We) do not have enough money to buy ice cream. ____**plural**____

● **Circle the subject pronoun that correctly completes each sentence.**

6. Jackie and (I)   me) saw the parade downtown.

7. (They)   Them) moved here from Iowa.

8. (Us   (We) were the only ones at the picnic.

9. (She)   Her) attends ballet class every Tuesday.

● **Write a possessive pronoun to replace the italicized noun phrase in each sentence.**

10. *My room* is painted turquoise. ____**Mine**____

11. Robert has returned *your backpack*. ____**yours**____

12. *The Smiths' car* has a flat tire. ____**Theirs**____

13. This soccer ball is *my brother's and mine*. ____**ours**____

● **Underline the compound subject in each sentence. Circle the subject pronouns.**

14. (He) and (I) watched the new movie last Tuesday.

15. The girls and (he) illustrated the poster.

16. My mom and (you) can ride together in the truck.

17. (They) and (I) are almost done with our chores.

● **Use your knowledge of suffixes to circle the correct meaning of each italicized word.**

18. *meaningful*   (full of meaning)   without meaning   a person who is mean

19. *guilty*   (full of guilt)   without guilt   a person who has guilt

20. *hopeless*   full of hope   (without hope)   a person who hopes

21. *builder*   full of building   without building   (a person who builds)

22. *cheerful*   (full of cheer)   without cheer   a person who has cheer

● **Write *simile* or *metaphor* to identify each description.**

23. The subway train was a roaring dragon. ____**metaphor**____

24. Her new dress looks like a frosted birthday cake. ____**simile**____

25. Cho's ring was a sparkling star on her hand. ____**metaphor**____

26. The sunset was as brilliant as a fireworks display. ____**simile**____

27. The unusual clouds were like white puffs of smoke in the sky. ____**simile**____

● **Write *yes* if the statement is true or *no* if the statement is false.**

28. It is a good idea to write down details before you write a description. ____**yes**____

29. You can organize details for a description in a graphic organizer. ____**yes**____

30. An idea web shows details organized in chronological order. ____**no**____

31. A five-senses chart includes sensory words. ____**yes**____

Assessment Book Answers • 85

CHAPTER 3 Post-test

• **Circle the personal pronoun in each sentence. Write *singular* or *plural* to identify the number of the pronoun.**

1. Place those books on top of (it).   singular

2. Mother and (he) will pick up Sam at noon.   singular

3. The coach will drive (them) to the game.   plural

• **Underline the pronoun in each sentence. Write *first person, second person,* or *third person* to identify the pronoun.**

4. The teacher asked me to erase the board.   first person

5. Mom could not find her.   third person

6. Would you like to serve on the committee?   second person

• **Circle the subject pronoun that correctly completes each sentence.**

7. (We) Us) cleared a path.

8. Thomas and (I) me) are learning Spanish.

9. (Them (They) take the bus to school.

• **Underline the compound subject in each sentence. Circle the subject pronouns.**

10. My mother and (I) fixed breakfast.

11. (They) and (I) will help set the table.

12. (He) and (she) don't know where the napkins are kept.

• **Underline the direct object in each sentence. Write a pronoun that can replace the direct object.**

13. The artist used the watercolors.   them

14. Mr. Sanchez invited Sarah and me.   us

15. The child sharpened the pencil.   it

• **Circle the possessive pronoun or possessive adjective that correctly completes each sentence.**

16. How old is (your (yours)?

17. (Theirs) Their) hasn't arrived yet.

• **Underline the pronoun in each sentence. Circle its antecedent.**

18. (Mrs. Kageyama) told Antonio to bring the pencil to her.

19. The three (boys) asked if they could join the group.

• **Circle the pronoun that correctly completes each sentence.**

20. The alarm clock woke Mother and (I (me).

21. Last week (I) me) went to the dentist.

• **Write a contraction that can replace the italicized words in each sentence.**

22. *I have* only now started my report.   I've

23. *We are* aware of the new time change.   We're

• **Circle the correct meaning of each italicized word.**

24. *peaceful*   (full of peace)   without peace   a person who has peace

25. *baker*   baked like   without being baked   (a person who bakes)

26. *lucky*   (full of luck)   without luck   a person who lucks out

• **Write *simile* or *metaphor* to identify each description.**

27. My paper cut stung like the bite of a wasp.   simile

28. This room is a disaster zone.   metaphor

• **Write *yes* if the statement is true or *no* if the statement is false.**

29. Idea webs can help you organize details for a description.   yes

30. You must always organize descriptions according to the five senses.   no

● **Read the paragraph. Answer the questions.**

Do you want to become stronger and more flexible? If so, then ballet might be the answer for you. Ballet is a classical dance that includes both strength and flexibility training. Through carefully controlled movements, the ballet dancer moves his or her body through space to music. These movements challenge the body to lift and flex in a variety of ways. Most ballet classes meet once a week. They can last from 30 minutes to 90 minutes. So, if you have the time and the desire, give ballet a try. You'll be stronger and more flexible for it!

1. What is the main idea of the paragraph?
   A Ballet is done through carefully controlled movements.
   B Many people need to become stronger and more flexible.
   C Ballet is fun.
   D Ballet is a good way to become stronger and more flexible.

1. (A) (B) (C) ⟨D⟩

2. Which sentence from the paragraph provides a detail about the timing of ballet classes?
   F You'll be stronger and more flexible for it!
   G Ballet is a classical dance that includes both strength and flexibility training.
   H They can last from 30 minutes to 90 minutes.
   J These movements challenge the body to lift and flex in a variety of ways.

2. (F) (G) ⟨H⟩ (J)
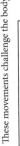

3. According to the paragraph why might a person take ballet classes?
   K to dance to music
   L to gain strength and flexibility
   M to take a class once a week
   N to control their movements

3. (K) ⟨L⟩ (M) (N)

Name _____ Date _____

Analyze Text: Main Idea and Details

Some test items might measure your ability to identify the main idea and details of a passage.

The test item might look like this:

Read the paragraph. Answer the question.

The Chargers are victorious for the fifth week in a row! The Chestertown High School varsity football team trampled the Litchfield Lyons by the score of 37 to 14 yesterday evening at Nelson Stadium. After the game junior quarterback Robert James was carried off the field on the shoulders of his teammates. "It's not over," said James to his team. "This year we go to state!"

1. What is the main idea of this paragraph?
   A Robert James doesn't weigh very much.
   B Nelson Stadium is good luck for the Chargers.
   C The Chestertown Chargers beat the Litchfield Lyons.
   D Robert James is a junior.

First read the paragraph carefully, trying to understand the ideas behind the words. Carefully read the question-and-answer choices. Ask yourself:
What is this paragraph mostly about?
How can I explain the main meaning of the paragraph in one sentence?
Which choices tell details, not the main idea?

You would then find the choice that best answers the question, rereading the paragraph if you are unsure. In the example you would choose answer C. You would choose answer C because
   • it best sums up the main meaning of the paragraph.
   • it is not a supporting detail.

Assessment Book Answers • **87**

CHAPTER 3

Name _____ Date _____

Description
Writing Prompt

Some tests check to see how well you write. The directions tell you what to write about. When you take a writing test, you can follow do the following.

1. Carefully read the directions.
2. Circle the important words.
3. Take a few minutes to plan your writing. You can draw or write to make a plan.
4. Write a draft.
5. Revise and copyedit the draft, but don't rewrite the whole thing.

- **Practice for a writing test by following the directions in the box. Plan your writing in the open box. Write your decription on a separate sheet of paper.**

What is your favorite kind of weather? Write a description of your favorite kind of weather as if you are standing outside experiencing it.

CHAPTER 3

Name _____ Date _____

Description
Scoring Rubric

- **In Chapter 3 you have written descriptions. Read the description that you wrote for the prompt on page 25. Then answer these questions.**

Description	Yes	No
Ideas		
Do I have a clear focus on one topic?		
Organization		
Did I include an informative beginning that names the topic?		
Does the piece have a body with logical organization?		
Is there a clear ending?		
Voice		
Do I use a tone appropriate for the audience?		
Word Choice		
Did I use vivid adjectives and verbs?		
Did I use similes and metaphors?		
Sentence Fluency		
Is there a variety of sentences?		
Conventions		
Did I check for correct grammar?		
Did I check for correct spelling?		
Did I check for correct punctuation and capitalization?		

CHAPTER 4 Pre-test

- **Circle each descriptive adjective. Write *proper* on the blank if the adjective is proper.**

1. My uncle has a (Swiss) watch. **proper**

2. A (loud) noise awoke me.

3. She carefully handled the (delicate) vase.

4. The (Egyptian) pyramids are built of stone. **proper**

- **Circle the demonstrative adjective in each sentence. Write *near* or *far* to identify the noun's location.**

5. Have you read (this) book? **near**

6. (These) pencils need to be sharpened. **near**

7. Can you tell if (those) hikers are from our group? **far**

- **Underline the adjective that tells how many in each sentence. Write *exactly* or *about* to identify how many it tells.**

8. Fifteen people won tickets to the movie's premiere. **exactly**

9. I watched as several squirrels fought over the breadcrumbs. **about**

10. A few leaves drifted on the water's surface. **about**

- **Circle the word or phrase that correctly completes each sentence.**

11. This test is (more difficult) most difficult) than the last one.

12. We went on the (scarier (scariest) ride ever at the water park.

13. My new book is the (most interesting) interestingest) one I've ever read.

14. This scarf has the (brightest) most brightest) colors of any on this table.

- **Circle the word or phrase that correctly completes each sentence.**

15. It seems as if there has been (less) least) sunshine this year than last year.

16. The team made (less) least) progress than their competition in the off-season.

17. I have the (less (least) time on my computer of anyone in my family.

- **Circle the descriptive adjective in each sentence. Write *after* if it is used as a subject complement; write *before* if it is in front of the noun it describes.**

18. The child's honesty is (admirable) **after**

19. The (likely) suspect was arrested at dawn. **before**

20. Do deer have (sharp) antlers? **before**

- **Circle the correct meaning of each italicized word. Use the meaning of the word's prefix to help you choose the correct answer.**

21. *disarranged*   (not arranged)   before arranging   arranged under

22. *prehistoric*   (before history)   not historic   less than historic

23. *underpass*   before passing   not passed   (a passage beneath)

- **Write *yes* if the statement is true or *no* if it is false.**

24. A dictionary is arranged in alphabetical order. **yes**

25. Guide words are usually found at the bottom of each dictionary page. **no**

26. A dictionary gives only one meaning for each word listed. **no**

27. A dictionary only lists those words used as nouns. **no**

- **Circle the time word in each sentence.**

28. Fold in the cream (after) the sugar mixture has cooled.

29. (First) cut the wire into six-inch sections.

30. Cut apart the remaining pieces (while) the glue dries.

31. (Before) the glue dries, add the labels.

Name _____ Date _____

CHAPTER 4 Post-test

- **Circle the descriptive adjective in each sentence. Write *proper* on the blank if it is a proper adjective**

1. We crept up the (creaky) stairs.

2. Mom cooked (Spanish) rice for dinner. **proper**

- **Circle the article in each sentence. Write the noun it points out.**

3. (The) first courthouse in California was built in Mariposa. **courthouse**

4. She placed (a) shiny apple on each desk. **apple**

5. Describe what (an) aardvark looks like. **aardvark**

- **Circle the demonstrative adjective in each sentence. Write *near* or *far* to identify the noun's location.**

6. Be careful you don't break (that) glass. **far**

7. (This) tile feels so cold on a winter morning. **near**

8. Do you know where I should put (these) papers? **near**

- **Underline the adjective that tells how many in each sentence. Write *exactly* or *about* to identify how many it tells.**

9. Many colorful balloons dotted the ceiling. **about**

10. A dozen pencils are in each box. **exactly**

- **Circle the word or phrase that correctly completes each sentence.**

11. The newspaper printed the name of the (safer (safest) road in the city.

12. I think spinach is (tastier) tastiest) than broccoli.

13. Last week was (more humid) most humid) than this week.

Voyages in English 4   Post-test ~ **Chapter 4** • **29**

- **Circle the word or phrase that correctly completes each sentence.**

14. Our team had the (better (best) practice ever on Tuesday.

15. The garbage smells (worse) worst) today than it did yesterday.

16. (Fewer) Less) birds nested at the pond this year than last year.

- **Circle the adjective used as a subject complement in each sentence. Write the noun it describes.**

17. Horseshoe crabs are (interesting) **crabs**

18. The child was (scared) of the dark. **child**

19. The surface of the stone is (smooth) **surface**

- **Circle the descriptive adjective in each sentence. Write *after* if it appears after the noun it describes; write *before* if it is in front of the noun it describes.**

20. The (unusual) book belongs to my grandfather. **before**

21. A (ghostly) image appeared in the doorway. **before**

22. The creature was only (imaginary) **after**

- **Circle the correct meaning of each italicized word. Use the meaning of the prefix to help you choose the correct answer.**

23. *underline*   not a line   a line before   (a line beneath)

24. *disprove*   (to prove not true)   to prove before   to view below

25. *preview*   not viewed   (to view before)   to view from below

- **Write *yes* if the statement is true or *no* if it is false.**

26. Guide words describe how to pronounce a word. **no**

27. A dictionary lists the meanings of a word. **yes**

- **Circle the time word in each sentence.**

28. The (next) step is to remove all the staples.

29. (Finally) display your sun catcher in a window.

30 • **Chapter 4** ~ Post-test   Voyages in English 4

© Loyola Press

CHAPTER 4

Writing Strategies: Time Words

Some test items might measure your ability to choose the time word that best fits a sentence.

The test item might look like this:

Read the paragraph. Find the time word that best fills the blank.

> The life cycle of a frog has roughly four stages. First, eggs are laid in water by a female frog to be fertilized by a male frog. Next, tadpoles hatch. These tadpoles have a tail and gills. Then the tadpole develops legs and webbed feet. _____, an adult frog loses its tadpole tail and develops lungs.

A. When

B. Before

C. Second

D. Finally

First read the paragraph carefully. Notice the order in which the ideas are written. Carefully read the sentence with the blank. In what part of the sequence does this idea take place? Then read each answer choice and ask yourself:

Does this word make sense in the sentence?

Does this word tell the correct order for the idea that follows?

Is it the best choice of all?

You would then choose the word that best fits the sentence. In the example you would choose answer D because

• it makes sense in the sentence and in the entire paragraph.

• it correctly names the last step in the life cycle of a frog.

• **Read the paragraph and answer the questions.**

> [1]Marco Polo, from Italy, was a world traveler in the 1200s. [2]He _____ traveled to China with his father when he was 17. [3]Soon he became a favorite of China's leader, Kublai Khan. [4] _____, the khan was sending Polo on missions all over Asia.

1. Which time word fits best in Sentence 2?

A second

B first

C next

D finally

1. Ⓐ **Ⓑ** Ⓒ Ⓓ

2. Which word in Sentence 3 is a time word?

F Soon

G became

H leader

J China

2. **Ⓕ** Ⓖ Ⓗ Ⓙ

3. Which time word or words best fits in Sentence 4?

K Now

L Yesterday

M However

N Before long

3. Ⓚ Ⓛ Ⓜ **Ⓝ**

Page 33

CHAPTER 4

How-to Article
Writing Prompt

Some tests check to see how well you write. The directions tell you what to write about. When you take a writing test, you can do the following.

1. Carefully read the directions.
2. Circle important words.
3. Take a few minutes to plan your writing. You can draw or write to make a plan.
4. Write a draft.
5. Revise and copyedit the draft, but don't rewrite the whole thing.

• **Practice for a writing test by following the directions in the box. Plan your writing in the open box. Write your how-to article on a separate sheet of paper.**

Think of something that you do to get ready for school, such as brush your teeth or eat breakfast. Write a how-to article that tells how to do it.

Page 34

CHAPTER 4

How-to Article
Scoring Rubric

• **In Chapter 4 you have written how-to articles. Read the article that you wrote for the prompt on page 33. Then answer these questions.**

How-to Article

	Yes	No
Ideas		
Did I write logical steps organized in paragraph form?		
Did I share my ideas in time order?		
Organization		
Does the article have a clear purpose shared in the introduction?		
Does the article have detailed, accurate instructions in the body?		
Does the article have a conclusion?		
Voice		
Are many sentences commands?		
Word Choice		
Did I use time words, such as *first* and *next*?		
Sentence Fluency		
Do the steps go smoothly from one to the other?		
Conventions		
Did I check for correct grammar?		
Did I check for correct spelling?		
Did I check for correct punctuation and capitalization?		

Pre-test

Name _____ Date _____

• **Circle the action verb in each sentence.**
1. Our class (performed) a play.
2. Mom (reads) my little sister a story each night.
3. I (ran) all the way home from school.
4. The rocket (zooms) into space.

• **Underline the being verb in each sentence. Some being verbs are formed with two words.**
5. They have been our neighbors for a long time.
6. Leonardo da Vinci was a great artist.
7. Who is that actor?
8. My story will be about dinosaurs.

• **Underline the linking verb in each sentence. Write the words it links.**
9. I am a gardener. — **I** / **gardener**
10. Dodge City was a famous town of the Old West. — **Dodge City** / **town**
11. The new players are they. — **players** / **they**
12. This football game is exciting. — **game** / **exciting**

• **Write the helping verb and the main verb in each sentence under the correct heading.**

	Helping Verb	Main Verb
13. My cousin can speak Japanese.	**can**	**speak**
14. The students must finish the test on time.	**must**	**finish**
15. The loud sounds are disturbing me.	**are**	**disturbing**
16. She is painting a watercolor.	**is**	**painting**

• **Underline the verb in each sentence. Write present or past to identify each verb.**
17. She walked home from the mall. — **past**
18. Roberto practices the new dive every day. — **present**
19. The coach outlined the next play. — **past**

• **Write the form of the verb in parentheses to complete each sentence.**
20. Angela **tried** the new dessert her mother made. (try—simple past)
21. Our class **will help** the kindergartners with their art projects. (help—future with will)
22. Grandmother **bakes** the most delicious cookies. (bake—simple present)

• **Write synonyms or not synonyms to identify the italicized words.**
23. She *ripped* up the picture after the eraser *tore* a hole in the paper. — **synonyms**
24. An *enormous* box sat on our *tiny* front porch. — **not synonyms**
25. I ran past the *shrubs* and jumped over the *bushes*. — **synonyms**

• **Write yes if the statement is true or no if the statement is false.**
26. A dictionary can only be used to find out word meanings. — **no**
27. A dictionary respelling shows another way to spell a word. — **no**
28. A dictionary entry can use dots to show where to break a word into syllables. — **yes**

• **Underline the compound subject or compound predicate in each sentence. Write subject or predicate to identify the compound part.**
29. Snow and ice covered the driveway. — **subject**
30. Janie plays piano and writes her own songs. — **predicate**
31. John and Melody drove to Connecticut. — **subject**

Name _____   Date _____

CHAPTER 5 Post-test

• **Circle the action verb in each sentence.**

1. The orange cat often (streaks) across the room without warning.
2. The gymnast (swung) up onto the bars.
3. The pine trees (grow) six inches each year.
4. An old truck (rumbled) past us.

• **Underline the being verb in each sentence. Some being verbs are formed with two words.**

5. Mr. Branson has been our principal for two years.
6. The sky is very blue.
7. Sandy and Michael were unhappy with their project.
8. I am sorry about the bad weather.

• **Underline the linking verb in each sentence. Write the words it links.**

9. Those birds are hungry.   birds / hungry
10. The frog is an amphibian.   frog / amphibian
11. Toby has been late every day.   Toby / late
12. The fastest runner was she.   runner / she

• **Underline the verb phrase in each sentence. Write the helping verb or verbs and the main verb under the correct heading.**

	Helping Verb	Main Verb
13. The leaves were falling from the trees.	were	falling
14. The colored pencils will be found in that box.	will be	found
15. The boulder had rolled down the hill.	had	rolled
16. I should have known the correct answer.	should have	known

---

• **Write present, present participle, past, or past participle to identify the italicized verb.**

17. After my sister *baked* the cake, I ate a piece.   past
18. The children are *beginning* to learn Spanish.   present participle
19. We *watched* the sunrise this morning.   past

• **Write the correct form of the verb in parentheses to complete each sentence.**

20. (break) Yesterday the baby   broke   her new toy.
21. (begin) My class is   beginning   to write a new story.
22. (choose) Have you   chosen   a new book to read?

• **Write the form of the verb in parentheses to complete each sentence.**

23. The bright sun   reflects   off the snow.
(reflect—simple present tense)
24. The boy   tripped   over the bump in the sidewalk.
(trip—simple past tense)

• **Write synonyms or not synonyms to identify the italicized words.**

25. I was *tardy* for school when my mom dropped me off *late*.   synonyms
26. After dinner we took a *stroll* along the *stream*.   not synonyms

• **Write yes if the statement is true or no if the statement is false.**

27. A dictionary respelling shows how to pronounce a word.   yes
28. Accent marks show what language a word is from.   no

• **Underline the compound subject or compound predicate in each sentence. Write subject or predicate to identify the compound part.**

29. The boy ran fast and leaped over the fence.   predicate
30. The woman and her daughter waited in line.   subject

CHAPTER 5

Sentence Structure: Subject/Predicate

Some test items might measure your ability to choose the subject or the predicate in a sentence.

The test item might look like this:

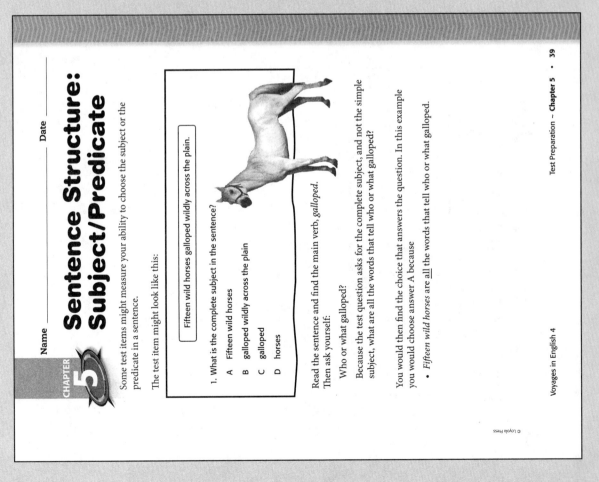

Fifteen wild horses galloped wildly across the plain.

1. What is the complete subject in the sentence?

A Fifteen wild horses

B galloped wildly across the plain

C galloped

D horses

Read the sentence and find the main verb, *galloped*. Then ask yourself:

Who or what galloped?

Because the test question asks for the complete subject, and not the simple subject, what are all the words that tell who or what galloped?

You would then find the choice that answers the question. In this example you would choose answer A because

• *Fifteen wild horses* are all the words that tell who or what galloped.

---

1. What is the simple subject in the sentence?

The funny clown juggled oranges.

A clown

B funny

C juggled

D oranges

1. (A) (B) (C) (D)

2. What is the complete predicate in the sentence?

The horse and buggy rambled over the bridge.

F horse

G The horse and buggy

H rambled

J rambled over the bridge

2. (F) (G) (H) (J)

3. What is the simple predicate in the sentence?

Mike happily roasted hot dogs.

K Mike happily

L Mike

M roasted

N roasted hot dogs

3. (K) (L) (M) (N)

Assessment Book Answers • 95

Page 41 (left)

CHAPTER 5

Persuasive Article Writing Prompt

Some tests check to see how well you write. The directions tell you what to write about. When you take a writing test, you can do the following.

1. Carefully read the directions.
2. Circle important words.
3. Take a few minutes to plan your writing. You can draw or write to make a plan.
4. Write a draft.
5. Revise and copyedit the draft, but don't rewrite the whole thing.

● **Practice for a writing test by following the directions in the box. Plan your writing in the open box. Write your article on a separate sheet of paper.**

Think of something that you think students should not be allowed to do in school, even though they are currently allowed to do so. Write a persuasive article explaining your point of view.

Page 42 (right)

CHAPTER 5

Persuasive Article Scoring Rubric

● **In Chapter 5 you have written persuasive articles. Read the article that you wrote for the prompt on page 41. Then answer these questions.**

Persuasive Article	Yes	No
Ideas		
Did I focus on one viewpoint regarding a specific topic?		
Did I work to convince the reader to share my viewpoint?		
Did I give reasons backed by logical evidence, such as examples?		
Organization		
Does my introduction state my point of view?		
Does the body give reasons that support my point of view?		
Does the conclusion sum up my point of view?		
Voice		
Does the article have a persuasive voice?		
Word Choice		
Did I use opinion words such as *should, ought, must, or believe*?		
Sentence Fluency		
Did I include a variety of sentences, including those with compound sentences?		
Conventions		
Did I check for correct grammar?		
Did I check for correct spelling?		
Did I check for correct punctuation and capitalization?		

CHAPTER 6 Pre-test

- **Underline the progressive verb in each sentence. Write *present* or *past* to identify the progressive form of the verb. Hint: the verb is formed by two words.**

1. Roberto is flying to Guam for vacation.   **present**

2. They were cheering for the team.   **past**

3. I was taking the dog for a walk.   **past**

4. Dave and she are waiting for the bus.   **present**

- **Underline the past perfect tense verb phrase in each sentence.**

5. They had worked for two hours before they took a break.

6. Maria had cleaned her room before she went to the mall.

7. My brother had applied to four colleges before he was accepted.

8. The doctor treated the patient after the patient had taken all the tests.

- **Complete each sentence by circling the verb that shows correct subject-verb agreement.**

9. I (is (am)) waiting for my friends.

10. My sister (is) are) knitting me a scarf.

11. This chair (do (does) not feel comfortable.

12. Several cars (was (were) parked on the street.

- **Write *there is, there are, there was,* or *there were* to complete each sentence. Be sure to capitalize the first word in a sentence.**

13. **There were** _____ five newborn puppies in the basket yesterday.

14. Right now **there are** _____ several hungry people in the cafeteria line.

15. **There is** _____ a glass of ice water on the counter right now.

- **Underline the adverb of time or place in each sentence.**

16. I left the book inside.

17. Sally feeds the birds daily.

18. I can't find my pencil anywhere.

19. Thomas often washes the dishes.

- **Underline the adverb of manner in each sentence.**

20. The lion roars fiercely.

21. The ball player swung at the ball wildly.

22. A trickle of water ran slowly down the window.

23. Snow fell silently throughout the night.

- **Circle the homophone that correctly completes each sentence.**

24. Did you bring (your) you're) roller skates?

25. The boys (rode) road) their bikes to the park.

26. Are those (knew (new) shoes you are wearing?

27. The movie starts in one (our (hour).

- **Circle the sentence in each pair that has been expanded with an adjective and an adverb.**

28. (The geese honked noisily as they flew through the blue sky.)
    The geese honked as they flew through the sky.

29. (A poisonous snake silently crawled under the bed.)
    A snake crawled under the bed.

- **Write *yes* if the statement is true or *no* if the statement is false.**

30. A haiku is a story about animals.   **no**

31. Haikus often describe something beautiful.   **yes**

32. A haiku is always five lines long.   **no**

33. The first and last lines of a haiku each have five syllables.   **yes**

Name _____ Date _____

CHAPTER 6 Post-test

● **Underline the progressive verb phrase in each sentence. Write *present* or *past* to identify it.**

1. Dad is cooking dinner tonight.   **present**

2. Jason and Pat were playing tennis.   **past**

● **Circle the present perfect tense verb phrase that correctly completes each sentence.**

3. The artist (has created) have created) a masterpiece.

4. The swallows (have returned) has returned) already this year.

● **Underline the past perfect tense verb phrase in each sentence.**

5. Before we ate dinner, we had played two card games.

6. After she had corrected the papers, the teacher handed them out.

● **Write the future perfect tense form of the verb in parentheses to complete each sentence.**

7. I **will have finished** _____ by evening. (finish)

8. Josh **will have cleaned** _____ his room by now. (clean)

● **Circle the verb that shows correct subject-verb agreement in each sentence.**

9. The hamster (was) were) running in the exercise wheel.

10. (Do) Does) you know how to get to the gym?

● **Write *there is, there are, there was,* or *there were* to complete each sentence. Be sure to capitalize the first word in a sentence.**

11. **There was** _____ a party at Jake's house last Friday.

12. Right now **there is** _____ a bird sitting in that tree.

Voyages in English 4   Post-test ~ Chapter 6   •   45

© Loyola Press

● **Write *time, place,* or *manner* to identify the italicized adverb.**

13. Suzy dances *gracefully*.   **manner**

14. You will find the book *here*.   **place**

● **Complete the chart by writing the correct form of each adverb.**

Adverb	Compares Actions of 2	Compares Actions of 3 or More
15. early	earlier	earliest
16. far	farther	farthest
17. soon	sooner	soonest

● **Circle the adverb that correctly completes each sentence.**

18. The squirrel ran (more quickly) most quickly) than my dog.

19. Jeff skates (more skillfully (most skillfully) of all the children.

● **Circle the word that correctly completes each sentence.**

20. They didn't see (no one (anyone) they knew.

21. The movie has a (good) well) cast of actors.

● **Circle the homophone that correctly completes each sentence.**

22. Who ate the last (peace (piece) of pizza?

23. (Their) They're) mittens are too big.

● **Circle the sentence in each pair that has been expanded with an adjective and an adverb.**

24. (The talented composer effortlessly writes music.)
The composer writes music.

25. We watched as the ball bounced off the window.
(We silently watched as the ball bounced off the glass window.)

● **Write *yes* if the statement is true or *no* if the statement is false.**

26. Haiku is a form of Japanese poetry that rhymes.   **no**

27. The middle line of a haiku has seven syllables.   **yes**

28. A haiku often creates a peaceful image from nature.   **yes**

46   •   **Chapter 6 ~ Post-test**   Voyages in English 4

© Loyola Press

CHAPTER
6
Editing Skills: Punctuation

Some test items might measure your ability to use correct punctuation.

The test item might look like this:

> 1. Choose the answer that shows the correct punctuation.
>
>   A   Will you go to the store with me.
>   B   Will you go to the store with me?
>   C   Will you go to the store with me:
>   D   Will you go to the store with me"

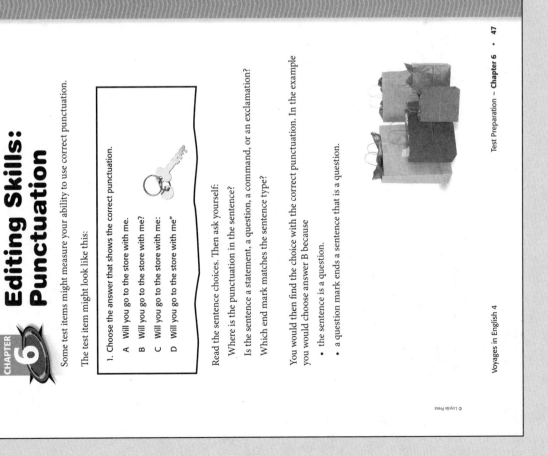

Read the sentence choices. Then ask yourself:

Where is the punctuation in the sentence?

Is the sentence a statement, a question, a command, or an exclamation?

Which end mark matches the sentence type?

You would then find the choice with the correct punctuation. In the example you would choose answer B because

- the sentence is a question.
- a question mark ends a sentence that is a question.

- **Choose the answer that shows the correct punctuation.**

1. Joyce _____ going to go skiing with us.

    A   isn't'
    B   isnt
    C   is'nt
    D   isn't

   1. Ⓐ Ⓑ Ⓒ ⬤D

2. F   You need markers crayons and paper.
   G   You need markers, crayons, and paper.
   H   You need, markers, crayons and paper.
   J   You, need markers crayons, and paper.

   2. Ⓕ ⬤G Ⓗ Ⓙ

3. K   The bus arrives at eight' o'clock.
   L   The bus arrives at eight oclock.
   M   The bus arrives at eight oclock'.
   N   The bus arrives at eight o'clock.

   3. Ⓚ Ⓛ Ⓜ ⬤N

CHAPTER 6

Fable Writing Prompt

Name _____ Date _____

Some tests check to see how well you write. The directions tell you what to write about. When you take a writing test, you can do the following.

1. Carefully read the directions.
2. Circle important words.
3. Take a few minutes to plan your writing. You can draw or write to make a plan.
4. Write a draft.
5. Revise and copyedit the draft, but don't rewrite the whole thing.

• **Practice for a writing test by following the directions in the box. Plan your writing in the open box. Write your story on a separate sheet of paper.**

Write a fable that has the following moral: When you are a friend, you will have a friend. Be sure that the characters are animals.

© Loyola Press

CHAPTER 6

Fable Writing Scoring Rubric

Name _____ Date _____

• **In Chapter 6 you have written fables. Read the fable that you wrote for the prompt on page 49. Then answer these questions.**

Fable	Yes	No
Ideas		
Did I write a story that teaches a life lesson?		
Did I include animal characters that have human characteristics?		
Organization		
Does the story have a beginning that introduces the main characters and setting?		
Does the story have a middle that describes a problem?		
Does the story have an ending that solves the problem and includes an explicit moral?		
Are the events told in chronological order?		
Voice		
Does the story have a lively voice?		
Word Choice		
Did I use natural language?		
Sentence Fluency		
Did I include a variety of sentences, including expanded sentences?		
Conventions		
Did I check for correct grammar?		
Did I check for correct spelling?		
Did I check for correct punctuation and capitalization?		

© Loyola Press

Name _____ **Date** _____

Pre-test

● **Circle the coordinating conjunction in each sentence. Underline the words it joins.**

1. The child smiled (and) laughed.

2. You can use paste (or) glue for this art project.

● **Write interrogative, imperative, declarative, or exclamatory to identify each sentence.**

3. The snake slithered under the car. **declarative**

4. Whose softball broke the window? **interrogative**

● **Circle the words that need capital letters in each sentence.**

5. (every)(july) we rent a house in (massachusetts).

6. (do) you know where (i) can find (mrs.) (robeson?)

● **Write yes if the title is written correctly or no if it is not.**

7. *Little House in The Big Woods* is my favorite book. **no**

8. He enjoyed reading the poem "By the Light of Day." **yes**

● **Rewrite each phrase, using the abbreviation for each italicized word.**

9. one *yard* of velvet, a hem of one *inch* **one yd. of velvet, a hem of one in.**

10. from *February* to *April* **from Feb. to Apr.**

● **Rewrite each group of words, using capital letters and periods.**

11. mrs j r perez **Mrs. J. R. Perez**

12. dr sally j mosley **Dr. Sally J. Mosley**

Voyages in English 4   Pre-test ~ Chapter 7 • **51**

● **Add commas to each sentence where needed.**

13. Maureen, your pet gerbil is cute.

14. The American flag is red, white, and blue.

● **Write possession or contraction to identify how the apostrophe is used.**

15. The cat's claws should be trimmed. **possession**

16. My little brother can't tie his shoelaces yet. **contraction**

● **Rewrite each line of the address correctly as it should look on an envelope.**

17. mrs c t duncan, 8980 w smithline drive, milwaukee, wisconsin, 53201

Mrs. C. T. Duncan

8980 W. Smithline Dr.

Milwaukee, WI 53201

● **Add quotation marks to show what each person said.**

18. "Try these on, said the shoe salesperson.

19. "The answer is ten," replied Devon.

● **Write a contraction to replace the italicized words in each sentence.**

20. *Do not* leave the lights on. **Don't**

21. Please tell me why you *will not* be at the game. **won't**

● **Revise this rambling sentence to make shorter, clearer sentences.**

22. My mother made muffins for breakfast, and they had walnuts in them, but Sherry does not like nuts, so she picked them out of her muffin.

Sample response: My mother made muffins for breakfast. They had walnuts in them.

Sherry does not like nuts, so she picked them out of her muffin.

● **Write yes if the statement is true or no if it is false.**

23. Nonfiction books and fiction books are arranged in order by the call number. **no**

24. Title cards are organized in alphabetical order. **yes**

52 • Chapter 7 ~ Pre-test   Voyages in English 4

Name _____ Date _____

CHAPTER 7 Post-test

• **Circle the coordinating conjunction in each sentence. Underline the words it joins.**

1. The cat yawned (and) stretched.
2. I like to read mysteries (or) science fiction.

• **Write *interrogative, imperative, declarative,* or *exclamatory* to identify each sentence.**

3. Where did you leave your shoes? _____ interrogative
4. Put on your gloves. _____ imperative

• **Circle the words that need capital letters in each sentence.**

5. (tony) (garcia) lives on (broadway) (avenue).
6. (bill) and (i) have piano lessons on (tuesday) with (mrs) (walker).

• **Write *yes* if the title is written correctly or *no* if it is not.**

7. "Remember the heroes" is a really good short story. _____ no
8. I just finished the book *By the Great Horn Spoon.* _____ yes

• **Rewrite each sentence, using the abbreviation for each italicized word.**

9. *Mister* Boyd lives in Tampa, *Florida.* Mr. Boyd lives in Tampa, FL.
10. Our school is on Elm *Street* in Ioka, *Utah.* Our school is on Elm St. in Ioka, UT.

• **Rewrite each group of words, using capital letters and periods.**

11. mr and mrs j f carlson Mr. and Mrs. J. F. Carlson
12. l m ruiz, u s citizen L. M. Ruiz, U.S. citizen

Voyages in English 4

• **Add commas to each sentence.**

13. We need milk, eggs, and flour for the cake recipe.
14. I know I am late, but that is my seat.

• **Write *possession* or *contraction* to identify how the apostrophe is used.**

15. I'm going to the mall with Sherilyn. _____ contraction
16. Did you see Harry's new bicycle? _____ possession

• **Rewrite each line of the address correctly as it should look on an envelope. Use capital letters, periods, and abbreviations where needed.**

17. doctor r j lewis, 7800 n fifth avenue, apartment 12, phoenix, arizona, 85010

Dr. R. J. Lewis

7800 N. Fifth Ave., Apt. 12

Phoenix, Arizona 85010

• **Add quotation marks and commas to show what each person said.**

18. The judge shouted "Order in the court!"
19. "It is getting late," Lupe pointed out.

• **Write a contraction to replace the italicized words in each sentence.**

20. We *must not* be late for our appointment. _____ mustn't
21. I *have not* seen your backpack. _____ haven't

• **Revise this rambling sentence to make shorter, clearer sentences.**

22. Yesterday I went skating at the park, and I forgot to look where I was going, and some sticks were in my way, and over I went!

Sample response: Yesterday I went skating at the park. I forgot to look where I was going. Some sticks were in my way, and over I went!

• **Write *yes* if the statement is true or *no* if it is false.**

23. Library catalog entries are arranged alphabetically. _____ yes

Voyages in English 4

CHAPTER 7

Word Study: Homophones

Some test items might measure your ability to understand homophones.

The test item might look like this:

Help the children put on _____ gloves.

1. Choose the word that correctly completes the sentence.

A they're

B there

C theer

D their

Read the sentence and word choices. Then ask yourself:

What does the sentence mean?

What does each word choice mean as it is spelled?

Which word is spelled in a way that makes sense in the sentence?

You would then choose the word that best fits the sentence. In the example you would choose answer D because

• the words *they're* and *there* are not adjectives.

• *theer* is not a word.

• the word *their* is a possessive plural adjective and it fits the sentence.

• **Choose the word that correctly completes each sentence.**

1. My little brother is _____ years old.

A too

B two

C to

D tooh

1. Ⓐ ⬤B Ⓒ Ⓓ

2. Turn _____ at the next stop sign.

F write

G wright

H rite

J right

2. Ⓕ Ⓖ Ⓗ ⬤J

3. Giselle did not want to _____ a dress.

K wear

L ware

M where

N were

3. Ⓚ Ⓛ Ⓜ Ⓝ

Name _____ Date _____

Expository Article Scoring Rubric

- In Chapter 7 you have written expository articles. **Read the article that you wrote for the prompt on page 57. Then answer these questions.**

Expository Article

	Yes	No
Ideas		
Does the article have a clear focus on one topic?		
Did I use factual information supported by research or personal experience?		
Organization		
Does the introduction include a topic sentence?		
Did I write a body of paragraphs that includes information that supports the topic sentence?		
Did I include a summarizing conclusion?		
Voice		
Does the article have a confident voice?		
Word Choice		
Did I use formal language?		
Sentence Fluency		
Did I use concise sentences?		
Did I use varied ways of providing information, such as expert quotations, statistics, examples, or explanations?		
Conventions		
Did I check for correct grammar?		
Did I check for correct spelling?		
Did I check for correct punctuation and capitalization?		

Name _____ Date _____

Expository Article Writing Prompt

Some tests check to see how well you write. The directions tell you what to write about. When you take a writing test, you can do the following.

1. Carefully read the directions.
2. Circle important words.
3. Take a few minutes to plan your writing. You can draw or write to make a plan.
4. Write a draft.
5. Revise and copyedit the draft, but don't rewrite the whole thing.

- **Practice for a writing test by following the directions in the box. Plan your writing in the open box. Write your article on a separate sheet of paper.**

Choose a topic that you have recently learned about in social studies or science, such as the Gold Rush or the life cycle of a butterfly. Write an expository article about the topic. Use your textbook if you need to do some research.

- **Write yes if the statement is true or *no* if it is false.**

5. Libraries are no longer useful sources because all information can be found on the Internet. ____ no

6. The librarian is a useful resource to help you find information. ____ yes

7. Since almanacs are up to date, it does not matter which year you use. ____ no

8. An almanac is a book of maps. ____ no

- **Circle the compound word in each sentence.**

9. The pilot positioned the plane on the (runway.)

10. The (lifeguard) watched the swimmers at the pool.

11. Does (anybody) want to play a game of soccer?

12. The beacon from the (lighthouse) shines for miles.

- **Write yes if the statement is true or *no* if it is false.**

13. An outline is a way to organize your notes onto one sheet of paper. ____ yes

14. First write capital letters, then Roman numerals when making an outline. ____ no

15. Use your outline as you write the introduction, body, and conclusion of your research report. ____ yes

16. The introduction should grab your audience's attention and tell what the report is about. ____ yes

---

Name _____ Date _____

Pre-test

- **Diagram the sentences.**

1. Albert's bicycle is red.

2. I often eat pizza.

3. The diamond is brilliant and dazzling.

4. Jessie and Martin quickly finished the puzzle.

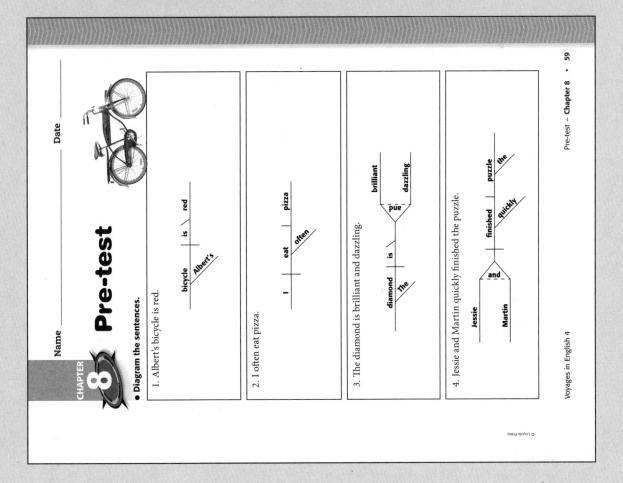

CHAPTER 8 Post-test

• **Diagram the sentences.**

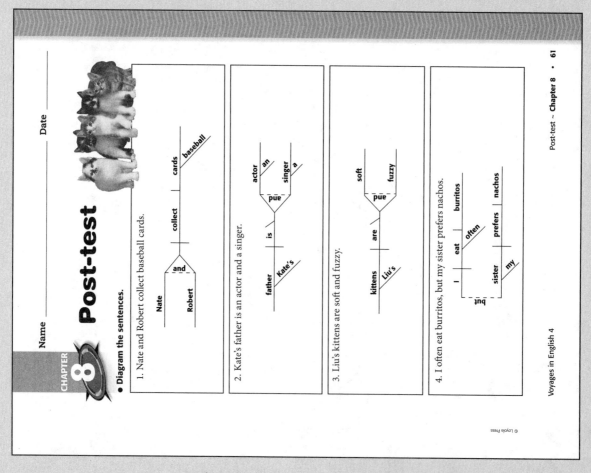

1. Nate and Robert collect baseball cards.

2. Kate's father is an actor and a singer.

3. Liu's kittens are soft and fuzzy.

4. I often eat burritos, but my sister prefers nachos.

• **Write yes if the statement is true or _no_ if it is false.**

5. The letters *.org* and *.gov* identify Web sites that are often reliable sources.   yes

6. The Internet contains the same amount of information as a library.   no

7. Almanacs are printed every year and contain recent facts.   yes

8. Encyclopedias give general information about a topic.   yes

• **Circle the compound word in each sentence.**

9. Her (brother-in-law) is a kind man.

10. A (blackbird) is making a nest in this tree.

11. This (handmade) quilt was a gift from my aunt.

12. A (lightweight) material was used in the car's construction.

• **Write yes if the statement is true or _no_ if it is false.**

13. The introduction of a research report is where you will use an outline the most.   no

14. A good way to set up an outline is to write a question for each Roman numeral.   yes

15. Under each Roman numeral write a regular number in front of each fact.   no

16. For your research report copy the words exactly as they appear in your outline.   no

CHAPTER 8

Spelling: Long Vowels

Some test items might measure your ability to identify the correct and incorrect spelling of words with long vowel sounds.

The test item might look like this:

> 1. Find the underlined word that is not spelled correctly.
>
> A   <u>screen</u> door
> B   starry <u>night</u>
> C   no <u>relefe</u>
> D   All correct

Read the phrases and study the underlined words. Then ask yourself:
Which words look right? Which words, if any, look wrong?
Which words sound right if I read them aloud? Which words, if any, sound wrong?
How might a wrong word be spelled correctly?

You would then choose the word that best fits the sentence. In the example you would choose answer C because

- *screen* and *night* look and sound right, but *relefe* does not.
- *relefe* should be spelled *relief*.

● **Find the underlined word that is not spelled correctly.**

1. A   not <u>compleet</u>
   B   stop <u>sign</u>
   C   <u>joke</u> book
   D   All correct

   1. (A) (B) (C) (D)

2. F   front <u>gate</u>
   G   <u>gleaming teeth</u>
   H   <u>stay</u> home
   J   All correct

   2. (F) (G) (H) (J)

3. K   green <u>mold</u>
   L   <u>fairy tale</u>
   M   <u>whight</u> stripes
   N   <u>sweet</u> treats

   3. (K) (L) (M) (N)

Research Report Scoring Rubric

Name _____ Date _____

CHAPTER 8

• In Chapter 8 you have written research reports. Read the report that you wrote for the prompt on page 65. Then answer these questions.

Research Report	Yes	No
Ideas		
Does the report have a clear focus on one topic?		
Did I give factual information supported by research that was gathered as notes?		
Organization		
Is there an introduction that includes a topic sentence?		
Is there a body that includes important main ideas supported by relevant details?		
Is there a summarizing conclusion?		
Did I include a simple list of sources (author and title)?		
Voice		
Does the report have the voice of an "expert"?		
Word Choice		
Did I use formal language?		
Sentence Fluency		
Does the report have varied sentence styles and lengths?		
Did I use varied ways of providing information, such as quotations, statistics, examples, or explanations?		
Conventions		
Did I check for correct grammar?		
Did I check for correct spelling?		
Did I check for correct punctuation and capitalization?		

Research Report Writing Prompt

Name _____ Date _____

CHAPTER 8

Some tests check to see how well you write. The directions tell you what to write about. When you take a writing test, you can do the following.

1. Carefully read the directions.
2. Circle important words.
3. Take a few minutes to plan your writing. You can draw or write to make a plan.
4. Write a draft.
5. Revise and copyedit the draft, but don't rewrite the whole thing.

• **Practice for a writing test by following the directions in the box. Plan your writing in the open box. Write your report on a separate sheet of paper.**

What is your favorite sport? Do research about the history of your favorite sporting event, and write a research report about its beginnings. Be sure to take notes and create an outline before your draft.

Name _____ Date _____

Cumulative Test

- **Circle the letter of the phrase that best completes each sentence.**

1. A personal narrative is _____ .
   a. writing that tells a story
   b. writing that reports facts about a topic
   c. writing in which you persuade the reader to do something

2. The introduction of a personal narrative should _____ .
   a. tell how the story ended
   b. grab the reader's attention
   c. be filled with details

- **Circle the complete subject. Underline the complete predicate.**

3. (Several bees) buzzed loudly.

- **Circle the direct object in each sentence.**

4. Mark cracked a (peanut)

5. My dog loves (pickles)

- **Circle the subject complement in each sentence. Write the subject it tells more about.**

6. The book was a (mystery)   book

7. His house is a (mansion)   house

- **Write yes if the statement is true or no if it is false.**

8. A time line organizes ideas from the most important to the least important.   no

- **Circle the word choice that gives the sentence a more precise meaning.**

9. My sister (brags) talks) about her many awards.

- **Circle the contractions in the sentence. Rewrite the sentence to make it more formal.**

10. (I'd) like to buy this book if (it's) not too expensive.
    I would like to buy this book if it is not too expensive.

- **Circle the letter of the phrase that best completes each sentence.**

11. A formal letter is used when people write _____ .
    a. about business matters
    b. to a good friend
    c. a report

12. To find out about a museum's hours and admission price, you would write _____ .
    a. a letter of complaint
    b. an informal note
    c. a letter of request

- **Write the plural form of each noun.**

13. woman   women

14. story   stories

- **Circle all the nouns. Write the noncount nouns on the line.**

15. (Sunshine) warmed the (puddle) of (water) on the (sidewalk)
    Sunshine, water

- **Underline the noun used as a direct object.**

16. The chef baked two pies.

- **Circle the noun used as a subject complement.**

17. Astronomy is an interesting (class)

- **Circle the letter of the sentence that is a compound sentence.**

18. (a.) The juice spilled, but I cleaned up the mess.
    b. The eggs are in the refrigerator behind the milk.

- **Write the following address as it should appear on a business envelope.**

19. Mr. Steve Davis, Director of Advertising; North Sea Sailing Company; 724 Glassel Avenue; Baltimore, Maryland 21202

    Mr. Steve Davis
    Director of Advertising
    North Sea Sailing Company
    724 Glassel Avenue
    Baltimore, MD 21202

© Loyola Press

- Circle the two words that are antonyms.
20. Anna is sometimes (early) but I am usually (late).

- Circle the letter of the choice that best completes each sentence.
21. A good description helps readers ___.
   a. follow a sequence of events
   b. understand synonyms and antonyms
   c. picture a person, place, or thing in their minds *(c circled)*

22. Using the five senses to describe something is an example of ___.
   a. poetry
   b. sensory language *(b circled)*
   c. formal language

- Circle the pronouns. Write each pronoun under the correct heading.
23. (They) explained where (you) could find (us) this afternoon.

First Person	Second Person	Third Person
us	you	They

- Underline the pronoun used as a direct object.
24. She took <u>him</u> to the hardware store.

- Circle the possessive adjective. Underline the pronoun contraction.
25. (Their) party is this evening, and <u>you're</u> invited to join us.

- Circle the pronoun. Draw an arrow to its antecedent.
26. The choir sang last night, and (it) was very entertaining.

- Circle the pronouns that correctly complete the sentence.
27. James and (I) me) will invite my sister to come with (we (us)).

- Circle the words that contain a suffix.
28. (teacher) (beautiful) preview (hopeless) uncover

- Write the two things that are being compared in the sentence.
29. Having been grounded, Todd's room became his prison.
   room and prison

- Circle the letter of the choice that best completes the sentence.
30. To organize details about things to do in the snow, it would be best to use ___.
   a. a five-senses chart
   b. an idea web *(b circled)*

- Circle the letter of the phrase that best completes each sentence.
31. A how-to article ___.
   a. recalls an event from the author's life
   b. tells the reader about a person or place
   c. teaches the reader how to do something *(c circled)*

32. In the body of a how-to article, each step is written as ___.
   a. a command *(a circled)*
   b. a question
   c. an exclamation

- Circle the articles.
33. (An) elephant waded in (a) pond by (the) thick bushes.

- Circle the form of the adjective that correctly completes each sentence.
34. Is walking (better) best) exercise than jogging?
35. Mickey had the (worse (worst)) spelling score in the class.

- Write the correct comparative form of the adjective in parentheses to complete the sentence.
36. This roller coaster is ___ more exciting ___ than the one we rode last summer. (exciting)

- Circle the letter of the adjective that correctly completes the sentence.
37. August had the ___ rainy days of any month this year.
   a. fewer
   b. fewest *(b circled)*
   c. least

- Circle the word that has the same meaning as the underlined words. Underline the prefix.
38. <u>arrange before</u>   disarrange   (prearrange)   rearrange

- Tell whether each word comes before or after *hinder* in a dictionary.
39. a. hiccup   before
   b. hinge   after
   c. historic   after

- **Underline the compound part of this sentence. Write *subject* or *predicate* to identify the compound part.**

50. The new player <u>caught the pass and shot for two points.</u> ____predicate____

- **Circle the letter of the choice that best completes each sentence.**

51. A good fable ____
   a. is a nonfiction story about people
   b. teaches the reader how to do something
   (c.) uses animal characters to teach a lesson

52. The problem is resolved in a fable's ____
   a. beginning
   b. middle
   (c.) ending

- **Circle the letter of the sentence that uses the present perfect tense.**

53. a. The family visits the park every summer.
   (b.) They have traveled to Asia several times.
   c. The park will be closed this weekend.

- **Write the future perfect tense of the verb in parentheses to complete the sentence.**

54. The boy ____will have finished____ his homework by this afternoon. (finish)

- **Circle the verb that agrees with the subject.**

55. There (is / (are)) many animals in the rodeo.

- **Complete the sentence by writing the correct form of the adverb in parentheses.**

56. My brother wakes up ____earlier____ than I do. (early)

- **Circle the words that correctly complete the sentence.**

57. The children work (good / (well)) together, and they don't ((ever) / never) argue.

- **Circle the homophone that correctly completes the sentence.**

58. My parents said (there / their / ((they're))) traveling to Arizona.

- **Circle the words and phrases that show time order.**

40. ((Start)) by cutting apart the pieces, and ((after that)) glue them into place.

- **Circle the letter of the phrase that best completes each sentence.**

41. People use persuasive writing to ____.
   ((a.)) convince others to think or act a certain way
   b. request information or a product
   c. give sensory details about a topic

42. A statement that can be proved is ____.
   a. an opinion
   b. a judgment
   ((c.)) a fact

- **Underline the verb phrase. Write the helping verb and the main verb.**

43. My parents are running in the race on Saturday.
   Helping Verb: ____are____   Main Verb: ____running

- **Underline the verb or verb phrase. Circle the word that identifies the verb's principal part.**

44. Several children <u>play</u> outside.   ((present))   past   present participle
45. I <u>have watched</u> this movie before.   ((past participle))

- **Complete the sentence by writing the correct form of *teach*.**

46. Have you ever ____taught____ someone how to play a game?

- **Rewrite the sentence, using the verb phrase *going to*.**

47. Maya walks to school.
   Maya is going to walk to school.

- **Circle the synonym for the underlined word.**

48. <u>dirty</u>   clean   ((filthy))   wet   idy

- **Use a dictionary. Write the pronunciation of each word.**

49. a. exclaim (**ĭk-sklām'**)
    b. applesauce (**ăp'-əl-sôs**)

- **Rewrite the direct quotation, using commas and quotation marks correctly.**

67. I do not know where your jacket is replied Zack.

"I do not know where your jacket is," replied Zack.

- **Write a contraction to replace each set of words.**

68. a. will not _____ **won't**

b. had not _____ **hadn't**

c. would not _____ **wouldn't**

- **Circle the letter of the choice that has been revised to make shorter, clearer sentences from the rambling sentence.**

69. a. Dennis opened the can and poured the soup into a pot and he heated it on the stove to make a tasty lunch.

(b.) Dennis opened the can and poured the soup into a pot. He heated it on the stove to make a tasty lunch.

- **Write _yes_ if the phrase is true or _no_ if it is false.**

70. A card catalog is organized in sequential order. _____ **no**

- **Circle the letter of the phrase that best completes each sentence.**

71. A research report _____.

(a.) gives information about a topic

b. tells a story from the writer's point of view

c. teaches a lesson

72. When you take notes for a report, you should _____.

a. copy the information exactly as you find it

b. never use another writer's ideas

(c.) write in your own words the information you find

- **Diagram the sentence.**

73. My favorite flowers are roses and lilacs, but Devon grows daisies.

- **Rewrite this sentence, using the adjectives _toasty, young,_ and _fascinating_ to expand it.**

59. The woman read a book in front of the fire.

The young woman read a fascinating book in front of the toasty fire.

- **Write _yes_ if the statement is true or _no_ if it is false.**

60. Haiku is a form of poetry that is written with a certain number of syllables. _____ **yes**

- **Circle the letter of the phrase that best completes each sentence.**

61. An expository article tells the reader about _____.

(a.) a topic

b. a poem

c. a character

62. Personal knowledge, human sources, and written sources are all ways to _____.

a. organize details for a main idea

b. find a topic for expository writing

(c.) find details about a topic

- **Rewrite the sentence, using abbreviations, periods, and capital letters where needed.**

63. mister a m smith lives on willow tree avenue.

Mr. A. M. Smith lives on Willow Tree Ave.

- **Rewrite this poem title and author's name, using capital letters and correct punctuation.**

64. under the chestnut tree by amy g griffin

"Under the Chestnut Tree" by Amy G. Griffin

- **Write the correct abbreviation for each word.**

65. a. pint _____ **pt** b. Wednesday _____ **Wed.** c. Alaska _____ **AK**

- **Rewrite the address, using commas and capital letters where needed.**

66. dr. janelle j. russell
1301 n. grugger ave. apt. a
san francisco ca 94166

Dr. Janelle J. Russell
1301 N. Grugger Ave., Apt. A
San Francisco, CA 94166

- **Write *encyclopedia*, *almanac*, or *atlas* to identify each research source.**

74. a. This source contains very recent facts.
almanac

 b. This source contains geographical and
 political features.
atlas

 c. This source contains general information
 about topics.
encyclopedia

- **Underline the compound words.**

75. The student found the answer in her notebook and wrote it on the chalkboard.

- **Write *yes* if the statement is true or *no* if it is false.**

76. An outline can be used to organize ideas for
a research report.
yes

Voyages in English
and
Exercises in English
Grammar Correlation Charts

GRADE 3

VIE Section	EIE Lesson
Sentences	
1.1	1
1.2	2
1.3	3
1.4	4
1.5	5
1.6	6
1.7	7
1.8	8
1.9	9–10
1.10	11
1.11	12
Sentence Challenge	13
Nouns	
2.1	14
2.2	15
2.3	16
2.4	17
2.5	18
2.6	19
2.7	20
2.8	21–22
2.9	23
2.10	24
2.11	25
Noun Challenge	26
Pronouns	
3.1	27–28
3.2	29
3.3	30
3.4	31
3.5	32
3.6	33
3.7	34
3.8	35–36
Pronoun Challenge	37

VIE Section	EIE Lesson
Verbs	
4.1	38–40
4.2	41
4.3	42
4.4	43
4.5	44
4.6	45–48
4.7	49–51
4.8	52–55
4.9	56
4.10	57
4.11	58
4.12	59
4.13	60
4.14	61
4.15	62
4.16	63
Verb Challenge	64
Adjectives	
5.1	65
5.2	66
5.3	67
5.4	68
5.5	69
5.6	70–71
5.7	72
5.8	73
5.9	74
5.10	75
5.11	76
Adjective Challenge	77
Adverbs and Conjunctions	
6.1	78
6.2	79
6.3	80
6.4	81–82
6.5	83
6.6	84
6.7	85
6.8	86
6.9	87
Adverb and Conjunction Challenge	88

VIE Section	EIE Lesson
Punctuation and Capitalization	
7.1	89
7.2	91–92
7.3	93–94
7.4	95
7.5	96–97
7.6	98
7.7	99
7.8	100
7.9	101
7.10	102
7.11	103–104
Punctuation and Capitalization Challenge	105
Diagramming	
8.1	106
8.2	107
8.3	108
8.4	109
8.5	110
8.6	111
8.7	112
8.8	113
8.9	114
8.10	115
Diagramming Challenge	116

VIE sections refer to 2006 edition, EIE lessons refer to 2008 edition.

GRADE 4

VIE Section	EIE Lesson
Sentences	
1.1	1
1.2	2–3
1.3	4–5
1.4	6
1.5	7–8
1.6	9
1.7	10
1.8	11
1.9	12
1.10	13
1.11	14
Sentence Challenge	15
Nouns	
2.1	16
2.2	17
2.3	18–19
2.4	20
2.5	21–22
2.6	23–24
2.7	25
2.8	26
2.9	27
2.10	28
2.11	29
Noun Challenge	30
Pronouns	
3.1	31
3.2	32–34
3.3	35
3.4	36
3.5	37
3.6	38
3.7	39
3.8	40
3.9	41
3.10	42–43
3.11	44
Pronoun Challenge	45

VIE Section	EIE Lesson
Adjectives	
4.1	46–47
4.2	48
4.3	49
4.4	50
4.5	51
4.6	52
4.7	53
4.8	54
4.9	55
4.10	56
4.11	57
Adjective Challenge	58
Verbs	
5.1	59–60
5.2	61
5.3	62
5.4	63
5.5	64
5.6	65–66
5.7	67–68
5.8	69–71
5.9	72
5.10	73
5.11	74
5.12	75–76
5.13	77
5.14	78
5.15	79
5.16	80–81
5.17	82
Verb Challenge	83

VIE Section	EIE Lesson
Adverbs and Conjunctions	
6.1	84–85
6.2	86–87
6.3	88
6.4	89
6.5	90
6.6	91
Adverb and Conjunction Challenge	92
Punctuation and Capitalization	
7.1	93–94
7.2	95
7.3	96
7.4	97
7.5	98
7.6	99–102
7.7	103–104
7.8	105
7.9	106
Punctuation and Capitalization Challenge	107
Diagramming	
8.1	108
8.2	109
8.3	110
8.4	111
8.5	112
8.6	113
8.7	114
8.8	115
8.9	116
8.10	117
Diagramming Challenge	118

VIE sections refer to 2006 edition, EIE lessons refer to 2008 edition.

GRADE 5

VIE Section	EIE Lesson
Nouns	
1.1	1–3
1.2	4
1.3	5
1.4	6–7
1.5	8
1.6	9–10
1.7	11–13
1.8	14
1.9	15
1.10	16
1.11	17–18
Noun Challenge	19
Pronouns	
2.1	20
2.2	21–22
2.3	23–25
2.4	26–27
2.5	28
2.6	29–31
2.7	32–33
2.8	34
2.9	35
2.10	36
2.11	37
Pronoun Challenge	38
Adjectives	
3.1	39
3.2	40
3.3	41
3.4	42
3.5	43
3.6	44
3.7	45
3.8	46
3.9	47
3.10	48–49
3.11	50
Adjective Challenge	51

VIE Section	EIE Lesson
Verbs	
4.1	52–55
4.2	56–57
4.3	58
4.4	59
4.5	60–64
4.6	65–66
4.7	67
4.8	68
4.9	69
4.10	70
4.11	71
Verbs Challenge	72
Adverbs	
5.1	73–76
5.2	77
5.3	78–80
5.4	81
5.5	82
Adverb Challenge	83
Prepositions, Conjunctions, Interjections	
6.1	84–87
6.2	88–89
6.3	90–92
6.4	93–97
6.5	98
6.6	99
Prepositions, Conjunctions, Interjections Challenge	100

VIE Section	EIE Lesson
Sentences	
7.1	101
7.2	102
7.3	103–105
7.4	106
7.5	107
7.6	108
7.7	109–110
7.8	111
7.9	112
7.10	113
7.11	114
Sentence Challenge	115
Punctuation and Capitalization	
8.1	116
8.2	117
8.3	118
8.4	119
8.5	120
8.6	121
8.7	122
8.8	123
8.9	124
8.10	125–126
8.11	127
Punctuation and Capitalization Challenge	128
Diagramming	
9.1	129
9.2	130
9.3	131
9.4	132
9.5	133
9.6	134
9.7	135
9.8	136
9.9	137
9.10	138
9.11	139
Diagramming Challenge	140

VIE sections refer to 2006 edition, EIE lessons refer to 2008 edition.

GRADE 6

VIE Section	EIE Lesson
Nouns	
1.1	1
1.2	2
1.3	3
1.4	4
1.5	5–6
1.6	7–9
1.7	10–11
1.8	12
1.9	13–14
1.10	15
1.11	16
Noun Challenge	17
Pronouns	
2.1	18–19
2.2	20
2.3	21
2.4	22–23
2.5	24–26
2.6	27–29
2.7	30
2.8	31
2.9	32
2.10	33–34
2.11	35
Pronoun Challenge	36
Adjectives	
3.1	37–38
3.2	39
3.3	40
3.4	41–42
3.5	43
3.6	44
3.7	45
3.8	46–47
3.9	48
3.10	49
3.11	50
Adjective Challenge	51

VIE Section	EIE Lesson
Verbs	
4.1	52–53
4.2	54
4.3	55–56
4.4	57
4.5	58–59
4.6	60–61
4.7	62
4.8	63
4.9	64–66
4.10	67–73
4.11	74
4.12	75
4.13	76
4.14	77
4.15	78
4.16	79
Verb Challenge	80
Adverbs	
5.1	81–83
5.2	84–85
5.3	86–87
5.4	88
5.5	89
5.6	90
Adverb Challenge	91
Parts of Sentences	
6.1	92–94
6.2	95–96
6.3	97–99
6.4	100–101
6.5	102–103
6.6	104–105
6.7	106–107
6.8	108
6.9	109–110
6.10	111–112
6.11	113
Sentence Challenge	114

VIE Section	EIE Lesson
Conjunctions, Interjections, Punctuation, Capitalization	
7.1	115–118
7.2	119–121
7.3	122
7.4	123–127
7.5	128
7.6	129
7.7	130
7.8	131
7.9	132
7.10	133
7.11	134
Conjunction, Interjection, Punctuation, Capitalization Challenge	135
Diagramming	
8.1	136
8.2	137
8.3	138
8.4	139
8.5	140
8.6	141
8.7	142
8.8	143
8.9	144
8.10	145
Diagramming Challenge	146

VIE sections refer to 2006 edition, EIE lessons refer to 2008 edition.

GRADE 7

VIE Section	EIE Lesson
Nouns	
1.1	1–2
1.2	3
1.3	4
1.4	4–7
1.5	8–9
1.6	10–12
Noun Challenge	13
Adjectives	
2.1	14–15
2.2	16–17
2.3	18–19
2.4	20–21
2.5	22–23
Adjective Challenge	24
Pronouns	
3.1	25–26
3.2	27–28
3.3	29–31
3.4	32
3.5	33
3.6	34
3.7	35
3.8	36–37
3.9	28
3.10	39
3.11	40
Pronoun Challenge	41
Verbs	
4.1	42–44
4.2	45–46
4.3	47
4.4	48–49
4.5	50
4.6	51–53
4.7	54–55
4.8	56
4.9	57
4.10	58–61
4.11	62–66
Verb Challenge	67

VIE Section	EIE Lesson
Verbals	
5.1	68
5.2	69–70
5.3	71–72
5.4	73–74
5.5	75
5.6	76
5.7	77
5.8	78
5.9	79
5.10	80
5.11	81
Verbal Challenge	82
Adverbs	
6.1	83
6.2	84–85
6.3	86
6.4	87–90
6.5	91–92
Adverb Challenge	93
Prepositions	
7.1	94–95
7.2	96–97
7.3	98
7.4	99
7.5	100
7.6	101
Preposition Challenge	102
Phrases, Clauses, Sentences	
8.1	103–106
8.2	107
8.3	108
8.4	109–110
8.5	111–112
8.6	113
8.7	114
8..8	115
8.9	116
8.10	117
8.11	118–122
Phrases, Clauses, Sentences Challenge	123

VIE Section	EIE Lesson
Conjunctions, Interjections	
9.1	124
9.2	125
9.3	126
9.4	127
9.5	128
9.6	129
Conjunctions, Interjections Challenge	130
Punctuation and Capitalization	
10.1	131–135
10.2	136–137
10.3	138
10.4	139
10.5	140
Punctuation and Capitalization Challenge	141
Diagramming	
11.1	142
11.2	143
11.3	144
11.4	145
11.5	146
11.6	147
11.7	148
11.8	149
11.9	150
11.10	151
Diagramming Challenge	152

VIE sections refer to 2006 edition, EIE lessons refer to 2008 edition.

GRADE 8

VIE Section	EIE Lesson
Nouns	
1.1	1
1.2	2
1.3	3
1.4	4–5
1.5	6
1.6	7–8
Noun Challenge	9
Adjectives	
2.1	10–11
2.2	12
2.3	13–14
2.4	15
2.5	16–17
Adjective Challenge	18
Pronouns	
3.1	19–20
3.2	21–22
3.3	22–24
3.4	25
3.5	26
3.6	27–28
3.7	29
3.8	30–33
3.9	33–34
3.10	35
3.11	36
Pronoun Challenge	37
Verbs	
4.1	38
4.2	39
4.3	40
4.4	41
4.5	42
4.6	43–45
4.7	46
4.8	47
4.9	48
4.10	49–51
4.11	52–57
Verb Challenge	58

VIE Section	EIE Lesson
Verbals	
5.1	59
5.2	60–61
5.3	62–63
5.4	64–66
5.5	67–68
5.6	69–70
5.7	71–72
5.8	73
5.9	74
5.10	75
5.11	76–77
Verbal Challenge	78
Adverbs	
6.1	79
6.2	80–81
6.3	82
6.4	83
6.5	84
Adverb Challenge	85
Prepositions	
7.1	86
7.2	87
7.3	88
7.4	89
7.5	90
7.6	91
Preposition Challenge	92
Sentences, Phrases, Clauses	
8.1	93–101
8.2	102
8.3	103–104
8.4	105
8.5	106–108
8.6	109
8.7	110
8.8	111
8.9	112
8.10	113–115
8.11	116–119
Sentences, Phrases, Clauses Challenge	120

VIE Section	EIE Lesson
Conjunctions, Interjections	
9.1	121
9.2	122
9.3	123
9.4	124
9.5	125
9.6	126
Conjunction, Interjection Challenge	127
Punctuation and Capitalization	
10.1	128–132
10.2	133–134
10.3	135
10.4	136
10.5	137
Punctuation and Capitalization Challenge	138
Diagramming	
11.1	139
11.2	140
11.3	141
11.4	142
11.5	143
11.6	144
11.7	145
11.8	146
11.9	147
11.10	148
Diagramming Challenge	149

VIE sections refer to 2006 edition, EIE lessons refer to 2008 edition.